B

lock Scheduling
A Collection of Articles

Edited by
Robin Fogarty

TRAINING AND PUBLISHING, INC.
Arlington Heights, Illinois

Block Scheduling: A Collection of Articles

Published by IRI/SkyLight Training and Publishing, Inc.
2626 S. Clearbrook Dr., Arlington Heights, IL 60005
800-348-4474 or 847-290-6600
Fax 847-290-6609
info@iriskylight.com
http://www.iriskylight.com

Creative Director: Robin Fogarty
Managing Editor: Julia Noblitt
Editors: Amy Wolgemuth, Troy Slocum
Proofreader: Sabine Vorkoeper
Type Compositor: Donna Ramirez
Formatter: Donna Ramirez
Illustration and Cover Designer: David Stockman
Book Designers: Michael Melasi, Bruce Leckie
Production Supervisor: Bob Crump

ISBN 1-57517-019-1
LCCCN: 96-75270

1710D-2-98PG
Item number 1396
06 05 04 03 02 01 00 99 98   15 14 13 12 11 10 9 8 7 6 5 4

$\Bigl($ontents

Block Scheduling
A Collection of Articles

An invasion of armies can be resisted, but not an idea whose time has come.—Victor Hugo

While block scheduling is not a new idea, it definitely is an idea whose time has come. Inspired by the reform movement of the nineties that focuses on the learner-centered school, educators search for ways to enable student learning. Among the innovations attracting attention is the idea of providing sufficient "blocks" of time for students to learn, and learn in authentic and purposeful ways.

By partitioning the school day into larger chunks of time, by looking at the concept of flexible, modular scheduling that accommodates learning, school faculties create a framework that favors the needs of the learner. Moving from the traditional "bell schedule" of 50-minute periods, schools choosing block scheduling are redesigning the periods of time into 90-, 120-, and even 220-minute blocks. As advocated by Sizer (*Horace's Compromise: The Dilemma of the American High School,* 1984) and Goodlad (*A Place Called School: Prospects for the Future,* 1984), the concept is rooted in concerns about creating sufficient time to immerse students in the learning experience.

Block scheduling is about teacher teams, clusters of students, and time to plan and learn.

In this collection, the articles are divided into four distinct sections, aptly labeled, What?, So What?, Now What?, and What Else? More specifically, *what* is block scheduling all about? (defining and describing); *so what* do we do? (implementation models); *now what* are the implications? (staffing and programming); and *what else* is there to consider? (related issues).

More specifically, in the first section, "What . . . is block scheduling all about?," the three articles define and describe the essence of block scheduling. The discussion moves from Carroll's conceptual purpose of "organizing time to learn" to images of block scheduling at work.

The second section, "So what . . . do we do?," is comprised of four articles that target implementation models. The discussions range from innovative scheduling for elementary schools to the Copernican model for high schools. This section ends with an invaluable set of guidelines for implementing block scheduling.

In the third section of articles, "Now what . . . are the implications?," concerns about programming and staffing are addressed. One piece discusses the instructional methods that are especially tailored to larger blocks of time in the classroom and curricular frameworks that provide holistic "chunks" of curriculum for relevant learning. Another article provides insightful ideas for building staff development time directly into the block schedule.

Finally, in the last section, "What else . . . is there to consider?," a study discusses student performance with block scheduling and with nonblock scheduling. In addition, Carroll revisits the Copernican Plan and evaluates it from the perspective of eight schools.

Each of the aforementioned sections is prefaced with a brief overview that serves as both an introduction and an abstract of the content of each article, providing the reader with a user-friendly synopsis. While this is by no means a comprehensive collection of the writings on the topic, the selected articles do provide a substantive look at the primary issues that surround the idea of block scheduling.

What?

All great ideas are controversial, or have been at one time.—George Seldes

B
lock scheduling is about the relationship between instructional time and learning. It's about structuring the school day in ways that favor students and foster learning. Rather than continue the seven-period-day slivers in which students are rotated every fifty minutes to another subject, another teacher, and often to another part of the building, advocates of block scheduling divide the day into bigger chunks of time.

These larger allotments of time allow students to concentrate their energies intensely on a single focus—the subject matter addressed during the block of time. In other words, the schedule itself encourages more involved, more active, and more student-initiated learning. To shed additional light on the idea of block scheduling, this first section is devoted to further defining and describing the concept.

As documented in the opening article by Joseph Carroll, interest in block scheduling dates back to the mid-1960s. Lending historical insight into the concept of "macro scheduling," the author recalls how the seeds of his "Copernican Plan" of block scheduling are grounded in a kind of "best practice" experience. Named for the Renaissance scholar Copernicus, the model challenges the traditional approach to school-day scheduling. While the article's focus is on the high school, readers across the K–college spectrum will find Carroll's discussion of great interest for its historical context and for the common sense evidenced in his thoughtful approach to the issues of children and learning. In addition, the author provides a practical plan and a comprehensive look at the change process.

Delineating the change process as experienced in one high school, Rebecca Shore discusses how personalization—"the single most important factor that keeps kids in school"—and Ted Sizer's theory based on this concept dictated her school's decisions concerning scheduling. The author hails block scheduling as perhaps the most significant among a number of recent innovations and concludes with a discussion of the benefits realized through the experience.

Roger Schoenstein provides the teacher's voice in a reflective piece about making block scheduling work. Closing this first section of articles that define and describe block scheduling, the article walks the reader through a number of practical concerns, anticipating and then answering the types of questions that teachers will raise. Beginning with how block scheduling works, the discussion touches on numerous issues—including the benefits of smaller classes, absentee students, advanced placement concerns, sequential courses, graduation credits, and coverage of content and school climate—and concludes with a balanced look at the results of four years of using block scheduling. In response to one final question—"Would you go back to a traditional seven-period day?—Schoenstein proclaims, "I'd never go back. . . . I just wish this had happened 23 years ago."

Block scheduling has been and is a controversial issue. Hopefully, these initial essays, with a bit of the history, some definitions, and a sampling of the questions and concerns, will serve to begin a healthy dialogue. Then, on to the second set of articles to find out more about the implementation process.

Organizing Time to Support Learning

by Joseph M. Carroll

The Copernican Plan is not about "block scheduling." It is about the relationship between time and learning.

My interest in this relationship began when I was assistant superintendent for research, budget, and legislation for the District of Columbia Public Schools in the mid-1960s. We initiated a remedial summer school for academically troubled students. For six weeks, these students studied math and English for four hours a day, five days a week—a typical summer program.

> **We may know a lot more about teaching than we do about how students learn.**

What was atypical was that we evaluated their progress carefully. Based upon traditional pre- and post-tests, average students' gains equaled the gains achieved in about two years in regular classes. The teachers' reports on the climate in the classroom, attendance, etc., were equally good. We were elated.

Then we asked if we can do this well in 30 four-hour summer classes in unairconditioned public schools, why can't we do better in our traditional 180-day regular programs? We thought of many possible reasons, but my only conclusion was we may know a lot more about teaching than we do about how students learn.

A QUIET EXPERIMENT

I followed up on this experience when I became superintendent of the Los Alamos Public Schools in New Mexico in the early

From *The School Administrator*, vol. 51, no. 3, March 1994, pp. 26–28, 30–33. © 1994 by the American Association of School Administrators. Reprinted with permission.

1970s. We offered students regular high school credit courses on a non-remedial basis as part of our summer school program. Each class met for four hours a day, five days a week, for six weeks, about 20 percent fewer total hours to complete a course than was provided under the school's traditional, 180-day schedule.

This disparity never surfaced, but it interested me greatly. The teachers were asked to use the same standards used during the regular year in grading their courses and to let us know whether the students could not meet the district's usual standards in this format.

Again the results were excellent and the teachers reported exceptionally good relations with the students. The "Coke breaks" were enjoyable and instructive. But what to do with this information? We seemed to have an answer looking for a problem!

The "problem" surfaced in the fall of 1982, when I was superintendent of the Masconomet Regional School District in Massachusetts. A tax limitation referendum passed in 1980 resulted in our district losing about one sixth of its teaching staff. Keeping the program intact was a serious problem.

Necessity breeds invention, and I decided to try to put into practice this "macro scheduling," as I had come to call it. In the fall of 1983, I distributed a long concept paper that I called "The Copernican Plan."

CHALLENGING TRADITION

Four hundred years ago, the Renaissance scholar Copernicus demonstrated the unsystematic movements of the planets could be systematically explained if one begins with the assumption that the sun, not the earth, is the center of the universe, as was then thought.

Unfortunately, this finding challenged basic, traditional teachings of the church and resulted in what was called the "Copernican Revolution." Indeed, the definition of "revolution" as social upheaval stems from the title of his book, *The Revolution of the Heavenly Orbs*.

Similarly, our Copernican Plan challenged tradition, the traditional organization of our secondary schools and particularly our high schools. Like Copernicus, the plan deals with facts and research that have been known for a long time, but which never seemed to make sense in the real world of schools. The Copernican problem was in the use of time, the daily and annual schedules.

What's wrong with the traditional secondary schedule? Plenty! The typical secondary school teacher must teach five classes a day for 180 days a year. Assuming an average class size of 25 students, a teacher typically deals with about 125 students each day in five classes, usually with three preparations and sometimes more than one discipline. A review of the research on effective instruction indicates the key concept is individualization. Teachers cannot deal meaningfully with every student every day under this traditional schedule.

> Teachers cannot deal meaningfully with every student every day under [the] traditional schedule.

Similarly, the student typically takes six classes each day, each packaged in periods of about 45 minutes, regardless of the subject. Assuming a seven-period day, a homeroom, and lunch, a typical student will be in nine locations pursuing nine different activities in a 6 $1/2$–hour school day. If the schedule includes physical education, he or she may have changed clothes twice and showered once.

This is a work schedule unlike any experienced either before or after high school or in the workplace. It produces a hectic, impersonal, inefficient instructional environment.

Nothing is wrong with the Carnegie-based schedule except that it prevents teachers from teaching well and students from learning well!

TIME REDEPLOYED

The Copernican Plan proposes many changes: interest/issues seminars; evaluation based on a mastery credit system; individual learning plans; multiple diplomas; a new credit system with two types of credits; and dejuvenilization of our high schools.

But the achievement of these changes—or any other of the many interesting changes proposed for our high schools—depends upon a fundamental change in the use of time. Classes can be taught in much longer periods—90 minutes, two or four hours a day—and which meet for only part of the school year—30 days, 45 days, 60 days, or 90 days. Students are enrolled in significantly fewer classes each day and teachers deal daily with significantly fewer classes and students.

The Copernican change in schedules is not an end; rather it is a means to several important ends. The most important of these are to improve vastly the relationships between teachers and students and to provide teachers and students with much more manageable workloads. In theory, improved teacher/student relationships and more manageable workloads should result in more successful schools.

> The Copernican change in schedules is not an end; rather it is a means to several important ends.

SPECIFIC FINDINGS

The Copernican Plan states: "Virtually every high school in this nation can decrease its average class size by 20 percent; increase its course offerings or number of sections by 20 percent; reduce the total number of students with whom a teacher works each day by 60 to 80 percent; provide students with regularly scheduled seminars dealing with complex issues; establish a flexible, productive instructional environment that allows effective mastery learning as well as other practices recommended by research; get students to master 25 to 30 percent more information in addition to what they learn in the seminars; and do all of this within approximately present levels of funding."

Most educators agree that to accomplish the above would be remarkable, particularly at the senior high school level. In 1983, when I first introduced the Copernican Plan, some research and a few non-traditional educational programs supported these concepts. The proposal generated many questions and much opposition at that time.

The critically important step I took was to arrange for a first-rate evaluation by a team from Harvard University that brought objectivity, competence, and credibility to our efforts. The evaluation addressed several key questions:

• Will students "burn out" in these much longer classes? (They won't.)

- Will teachers "burn out" under this type of schedule? (They don't.)
- Will students learn as much in about 25 percent less time per course? (They did, and they also completed many more courses.)
- Will students retain what they learned as well under a Copernican schedule as they do under a traditional schedule? (They do.)
- And by taking a course in a more intense schedule, will students develop the in-depth, problem-solving skills as well as they do (allegedly) in a traditional 180-day schedule? (They did significantly better.)

> While significant differences occurred in the results under different Copernican formats, every school benefited.

As a result, the Harvard team stated: "Implementing a Copernican-style schedule can be accomplished with the expectation of favorable pedagogical outcomes."

That statement now has been tested in an evaluation of seven quite different high schools in four states and one Canadian province. These seven schools use six different Copernican scheduling formats.

The common evaluations are all outcomes-based, measuring student conduct and academic mastery. The evaluative design compares the results achieved at each school with those achieved under a Copernican schedule. In every case, the results solidly favored the Copernican structure and the results were statistically significant at consistently high levels of confidence.

While significant differences occurred in the results under different Copernican formats, every school benefited from the change. Some formats are more effective than others. The orders of magnitude of these improvements in conduct and increases in academic mastery are educationally spectacular.

These results, however, are not really surprising. They are consistent with the research. The Harvard team was right. Any school can implement a Copernican-type schedule with the expectation of pedagogical gain.

THE CHANGE PROCESS

Schools, particularly high schools, don't change much. Why?
Many books and articles address that question. Most answers
follow a pattern: strategic planning;
beliefs analysis; district vision; school
vision; scope and sequence; objectives;
outcomes; authentic tasks; assessing authentic tasks. The total quality movement
appears to undergird these efforts.

> **Change in all of these
> schools was far more
> "product" dominated
> than usual.**

These are useful approaches. Cer-
tainly a common vision, a good plan, and
strong support of all stakeholders are most desirable. A few
messages from this decade of Copernican experiences add to
this large body of professional literature concerning change. In-
terestingly, they differ considerably from the current conventional wisdom about how to change schools.

These messages include:

Process Is Not Product

Three of the seven schools evaluated plus Masconomet followed
more traditional practices in achieving change. Nonetheless, all
showed significant improvements in student performance; indeed they had the best total results. (And one is hard pressed to
find evidence of even modest student improvement as a result
of other current efforts at educational reform.)

Only two schools had special grants to develop their program. Six schools had only the normal district resources. Five of
the seven schools and Masconomet had a solid majority of
teachers supporting the proposed change. Three did not and
their results were among the best of this group. The difference
appears to be that change in all of these schools was far more
"product" dominated than usual, and this emphasis directed
the process.

Based on conversations over many years with hundreds of
educators from schools planning to change, the change process
itself dominates the scene far too often and there is an assumption that whatever is done or not done will improve the school.

Successful Change Must Be Research-Based and Systemic

A surprise: The school with the poorest process and least preparation of staff had the best overall results. The school with the best staff development program, which used an inclusive, multi-year planning process, had the poorest results, although the school's total program improved over results achieved under its traditional structure. The differences were significant. Why?

The answer seems to come from W. Edwards Deming and total quality management concepts. Deming refers to the 85/15 rule: 85 percent of the problems are in the system and only 15 percent are in the people or subgroups. A Copernican change is systemic; it impacts all of the students and teachers in every class every day. However, the traditional schedule is also systemic. The difference is that no research supports continuing with the Carnegie unit; it actually impairs effective instruction. The Copernican structure is research-based and fosters more effective instruction.

The message: The process must be centered on developing a system that is based on sound instructional research and upon research-based evaluations of programs that have demonstrably improved student performance.

Leadership Is Critical

All of these schools had good leadership, leaders with a clear "feel" for the problems with the present system who were determined to make improvements. They seemed to understand that while it is possible to change without improving, it is impossible to improve without changing.

Too many schools and school districts are waiting for a "textbook process" to be completed. Too often the process becomes a vehicle to slow or avoid substantive change. Aristotle said: "In practical matters the end is not mere speculative knowledge of what is to be done, but rather the doing of it." The expectation of action to plan and also a plan of action based upon solid research is the major contribution the superintendent and other administrators can provide their staff.

Change the Whole School at Once

The school is the productive unit in education. Avoid pilot programs and schools-within-a-school. Schools, like people, seem to have an in-built rejection mechanism that is disruptive and subverts change. Pilot programs threaten those who do not want to be involved, and what threatens them most is that the program will be considered successful and they may have to change!

Evaluate, Evaluate, Evaluate

The major problem in plans to change schools is the failure to plan the evaluation as an integral part of the program and to evaluate in terms of student outcomes. Use competent outside evaluators who can provide professional expertise not readily available in most schools. They have more credibility because they are not part of the school's administrative structure and appear more objective.

> Schools, like people, seem to have an in-built rejection mechanism that is disruptive and subverts change.

Change always generates critics. In a couple of years, critics will be looking for "solid data." Lacking this, the program could be terminated. Many good professionals will advise superintendents not to initiate academic evaluations until the new program is being implemented properly. This could take several years.

This experience does not support that position. The key political and professional question is whether the new program is improving the education of students, based on measures that the profession and the public will accept as "solid." That is a reasonable question. Be prepared to answer that question. Observe carefully. Nothing, absolutely nothing, has happened in education until it has happened to a student. Evaluate!

A Caveat: Beware of the Gifted Opposition

Teachers and parents associated with honors courses are usually pleased with the current program and see no reason to change. Consequently, the group that most often leads the opposition are teachers and parents associated with the higher-performing tracks, the honors students. For similar reasons, schools viewed locally as very good are harder to change than those that are viewed as troubled.

Two of the seven schools included in my studies, as well as Masconomet, encountered this source of opposition, and a number of other schools also have reported the honors parents as a source of opposition. Honors parents and teachers are stakeholders in the process, but they see their stake in retention of the program under which their children prosper. Try to improve their understanding. Able students do better under a Copernican structure. But remember, there are many more "gifted parents" than "gifted students"!

Determine How Much Change a School Community Can Absorb

Don't try to make several major changes at once. There is usually a logical sequence in pacing the changes you try to implement. Limit change, and sequence the changes carefully.

RIPE FOR CHANGE

Schools are political entities. The nation has serious educational problems and depends upon about 15,000 school districts and 100,000 individual schools to identify these problems and implement improvements. This non-system is not capable of meeting the nation's requirements for improved student performance.

Probably we will see little substantive improvement until schools can operate under a substantially different political structure. But lacking that change, a Copernican revolution in the nation's secondary schools financially is feasible and will do much to address our nation's educational problems. In doing that, it also will address the local school district's needs. Most importantly, it will result in something very good happening to students. Remember, nothing has happened in education until it happens to a student.

How One High School Improved School Climate

by Rebecca Shore

ersonalization is the single most important factor that keeps kids in school," according to Ted Sizer, founder and director of the Coalition for Essential Schools.

Huntington Beach High School is not a Coalition School. While class sizes throughout the state of California lead the country in the too-many-kids-per-teacher category, the situation in Huntington Beach is particularly dismal. After more than a decade of declining enrollment, the district contract now allots 180 students per teacher per day—far beyond Sizer's recommended limit of 80 students per teacher day!

> A personalized education is one where students are known by adult professionals in the school.

Nevertheless, three years ago the staff at Huntington set out to test Sizer's theory. Since 1991, the school has gone from being generally regarded as a "nonperforming" school to being selected as a California Distinguished School. A number of programs contributed to Huntington's dramatic turnaround.

KNOW YOUR STUDENTS

A personalized education, according to Sizer, is one where students are known by adult professionals in the school. Huntington Beach enrolls approximately 2,000 students—9th through 12th grades—with 37–40 students per class. It is roughly 34 percent minority, and like many high schools in the country, has

From *Educational Leadership*, vol. 52, no. 5, May 1995, pp. 76–78. © 1995 by the Association for Supervision and Curriculum Development. Reprinted with permission.

seen an increase in violence and suspendable behaviors over the years. Previous administration had taken the usual steps to curb unacceptable behaviors, such as discontinuing evening activities like dances and instituting a stricter dress code.

> The small percentage of the student population that was engaging in unacceptable behaviors was also less than successful in their classes.

In 1991, the new administration looked the situation over and, as one might predict, found that the small percentage of the student population that was engaging in unacceptable behaviors was also generally the same population that was less than successful in their classes as reflected in their report cards. This revelation led to the development of our first program.

The vice principal of supervision, school psychologist, nurse, and community outreach liaison all created "hot lists," if you will, of students viewed as not on track to graduate due to some type of behavior problem. In addition, all teachers jotted down the names of their top 10 students who appeared to need extra attention. The district office provided a list of all students with three or more Fs on their last report card. Using the various lists, we then cross-referenced the names and made efforts to get to know these kids by name.

First, we initiated an adopt-a-kid program by matching up adult volunteers on campus with one or two students of their choosing from the list. The goal? Lend a listening ear for the student. Give information where needed and support or advice when asked. As every student has a distinct learning style, every adult has a unique personality style, and we attempted to match these. The adults met with the sudents before school, after school, at lunch, or during class, when appropriate. To ensure frequent contact, several of the teachers made the student their class aide. Although some adults met with their students less frequently, at least one adult on campus was able to greet the student by name.

At the same time, we formed a weekly group to discuss the progress of students on the list. Members of our group included the vice principal, assistant principal, psychologist, nurse, community outreach liaison, and other staff. Our group functioned much like a student study team, but our focus was not limited to special education students. As a result, all of the student services personnel kept in close communication and were able to compare notes, ensuring that the left hand knew what the right hand was doing.

Honor Thy Students

Each quarter the principal presented a Most-Improved Student Award, based on teachers' suggestions. The principal called these students out of class to personally present the awards: a key chain with their name on it (provided by our parent/ teacher association), a certificate, and a letter for their parents. In addition, the principal read the personal comments the teacher had written about the student. Many of the students on the adopt-a-kid list went on to become most-improved students.

> At student forums, any student could discuss school policy and activities or voice any complaints.

At the same time, school administrators continued the Student of the Month program, which honored outstanding students by placing their names on the school marquee and mentioning them in the principal's newsletter. We also initiated an Athlete of the Month program.

At student forums, which met twice a month at lunch in the principal's conference room, any student could discuss school policy and activities or voice any complaints. By having the vice principal chair the forum, the school showed students that their ideas were valued and worthy of administrative time.

TAKE A STAND AGAINST VIOLENCE

A yearlong green-ribbon campaign, initiated by the principal, promoted awareness of and expressed a nontolerance position toward school violence. This program was structured after the red-ribbon campaign, which designated a weeklong anti-drug awareness program. Every Tuesday, staff and students wore green ribbons to show their anti-violence stance. Ribbons were not passed out en masse, however; students had to request them from the front office. The response to the voluntary program was phenomenal. Within a month, students were donning the green ribbons—everywhere from their hair to their shoelaces.

In another effort, the principal convened a panel to discuss the increase in violence in the community. The panel included a juvenile court judge, a probation officer, a local detective, local police officers, and a mother whose son had been killed by gang gunfire. The principal organized a period-by-period school assembly (to ensure a smaller audience for the question-and-answer period). As a result of this candid discussion, students were empowered with first-hand knowledge about how illegal and violent acts are dealt with in the justice and penal systems. They were also touched by a personal account of the pain of senseless violence.

> With block scheduling, teachers see only two or three classes each day but for longer periods of time, thereby reducing the daily load.

TRY BLOCK SCHEDULING

Perhaps the most significant change that emerged from all of these efforts occurred during the 1993–94 school year. The staff at Huntington voted to try block scheduling. Accepting that they had no control over the 180 students each teacher was responsible for, they recognized that they could change the context in which they saw those students. With block scheduling, teachers see only two or three classes each day but for longer periods of time, thereby reducing the daily load to closer to 80. The longer periods of time, in addition, promote a more personalized environment.

The staff also instituted a tutorial period at the beginning of the block days, 30 minutes during which any student with a question could go to any teacher for one-on-one help. This sytematic change was a dramatic departure from the traditional schedule—the only one most of these veteran teachers had known.

REALIZE THE BENEFITS

Who's to say which of these programs was the most influential in curbing violence and suspendable offenses at Huntington

Beach High School. One thing's for sure, climate improved each year. For example:

• The school had the lowest explusion rate (only one) and suspension rate in the entire district for 1992 and 1993.

• Of the students on the "hot list," 51 percent improved their grade point averages in both the following years.

• During 1993–94, the entire list was reduced by 50 percent from the very start! (This was proabably a result of tutorial and block scheduling.)

At the same time, on the annual senior survey, 12th graders gave Huntington a higher rating than that of any senior class in the district. (The district includes six comprehensive high schools and one continuation school.) This was a first for Huntington! Test scores also rose, probably a reflection of the greatly improved climate around campus.

At the spring dance, held on a boat last year, the ship personnel commented that of all of their school groups that year, Huntington students had been the best behaved.

It is now common to see all school administrators out and about campus between classes, talking to students and calling them by name. Students and staff are generally smiling and greet one another with a "Hi, so-and-so." One staff member commented that 1994 was the best year he could remember in 18 years at the school. Another said this is the first time in 14 years that she's felt safe in a school assembly with the entire student population present.

Huntington accomplished all of these programs with no grants, no extra funding, and no additional manpower. These simple efforts to personalize the school experience led to dramatic improvements. The problems we faced, however, are not unique. Other schools willing to invest the time can accomplish the same results.

Author's note: For more information on any of these programs, call (714) 536-2514 or write to Huntington Beach High, 1905 Main St., Huntington Beach, CA 92648.

Making Block Scheduling Work

by Roger Schoenstein

Since Wasson High School, in Colorado Springs, Colorado, went to the block schedule, we've been asked questions by educators from all around the country. This is an effort to respond to some of the most frequent ones, but it's definitely not an "official" response; these are my own opinions:

HOW DOES YOUR BLOCK SCHEDULE WORK? Our students take four 90-minute classes each day, five days a week. Courses that used to run for a full year of 50-minute clsses now run for half a year of 90-minute classes. This is alternately known as the concentrated model, intensive model, 4 x 4 model, straight-block model, or four-block model. We teach three classes of 25 to 30 students each, totaling 75 to 90 a day; before, we were teaching five classes of around 30 students each, 150-plus a day.

The difference is dramatic. Having only 75 students, combined with the longer 90-minute classes, I know each student much better. I get a clearer sense of what she looks like when her parents have been fighting again, or that he's been closing late at the fast food place and not sleeping enough. As a teacher of block English classes, I have students writing much more frequently—obviously, since we now have 18 weeks instead of 36. But I now carry home 75 essays from three block classes, instead of 150

> Having only 75 students, combined with the longer 90-minute classes, I know each student much better.

From *The Education Digest*, February 1995, pp. 15–19. © 1995 by The Education Digest. Reprinted with permission.

from five traditional classes; I have half the essays to read at any one time.

If I teach some nine-week courses, my total number of students for the year could be more than 150, but during any term the total number of students will still be 75 to 90. As a foreign language teacher, my totals are often considerably under 150 a year. My Level I students will continue on to take Level II with me the same year. Many of my students have me for two year-long courses in a given year, so my yearly total will be 120 or 130, still with 75 to 90 in any one term.

HOW WILL A BLOCK SYSTEM LOWER THE CLASS SIZE?

It might not, depending on your current building schedule. We moved from a daily schedule of seven 50-minute periods. The block system has four 90-minute periods. Teachers teach three classes, with one 90-minute planning period.

Teaching longer time with the same number of students gave us smaller classes.

We went from 250 teaching minutes a day (5×50) to 270 (3×90). Teaching longer time with the same number of students gave us smaller classes. But that was our experience. We bought smaller classes by adding minutes to our instructional day.

It all depends on the schedule you're changing from when you restructure. A fringe benefit of the extra 20 minutes of instruction each day by each staff member was released time for staff development days. Once a month, we close school and talk—a critical component of school change, especially in the first one or two years. The extra time our students attend classes the rest of the month still meets our state's mandated minimum of 1,080 hours of instruction per year.

WON'T AN ABSENT STUDENT MISS SO MUCH WORK IN A BLOCK CLASS THAT HE'LL NEVER CATCH UP?

Students absent from block classes do miss more in each class. A student absent the whole day, however, misses four classes instead of six or seven. When he returns, he's missed a lot in each class, but he needs to track down only four teachers.

The nature of the interaction in the classroom itself is also an important factor in the issue of student absence. In a 90-

minute class, there ought to be time for me to meet with the student in the room, during the class period—to fill him in on what he's been missing. For the soccer player missing last period tomorrow because of the game, the same applies, only I need to met with him in class the day before. "You'll be gone tomorrow; we'll be doing so-and-so."

> In the past, only seniors completed the requirements to enter our AP classes, but acceleration now gives juniors this opportunity.

A final help for my absent students comes from their base groups in classes involved in cooperative learning activities. My students will often start with their group to find out what they missed, since part of the entire group's grade depends on the student keeping up. It's not an answer to the whole issue, but it can make it much easier for the student to find out what he missed if he starts with the rest of his group first.

HOW DO YOUR ADVANCED PLACEMENT CLASSES WORK?

Prior to restructuring, AP classes needed extra out-of-school meetings on weekends or evenings to get adequate preparation for AP exams. Classes lasted a full year and offered two credits. AP classes now last three nine-week terms, and students earn two credits. They run during terms two, three, and four, and students take one of various nine-week electives in their first term before their AP class starts.

The specter of a senior taking four AP classes comes to mind at this point: four AP classes and that's it—grim! That could still occur, but more AP students are taking AP Calculus or AP Biology, for example, as a junior, since they can accelerate and take two years of math or two years of science in their sophomore year. In the past, only seniors completed the requirements to enter our AP classes, but acceleration now gives juniors this opportunity.

HOW DO YOU DEAL WITH THE GAP IN SEQUENTIAL COURSES, SUCH AS FOREIGN LANGUAGE?

If a student takes first-year Spanish in the fall of his sophomore year, and then does not continue into second-year in January, and also does not get it scheduled until the spring of the following year, that full-year gap is not good. We worried a lot about the gap before making the change.

The gap is still not good, but we overestimated the problem. The key is to determine exactly where it causes problems. Our solution has been primarily one of scheduling. The student just wanting Spanish 1 should start in January and continue in September with Spanish 2. Starting Spanish 1 in September builds in a gap at the outset. Our old schedule created many situations where students were stuck with forced choices: "You want second-year French and Chamber Singers, but they're the same period—you'll have to pick." We did that too often to kids before we restructured.

> We are also seeing students taking multiple languages, which was virtually impossible before.

We still schedule in gaps where we don't want to, but it's much better to have the student take the class, even with a gap, than have to choose. The gap occurs when students only want one year of a language in a given school year. But we also have students taking two years back-to-back, especially first- and second-year, where we recommend doubling up in foreign language. These students are very strong when they hit third-year—taking two levels in the same year gives them a strong foundation without diluting the experience over two years' time.

We are also seeing students taking multiple languages, which was virtually impossible before. A student can accelerate and finish a four-year sequence in Spanish in less than four school years, true. But instead of losing him as a language student, we keep him when he starts first-year French or Latin. It's a real plus we hadn't fully anticipated when we restructured.

WHAT ABOUT RETENTION IF THE STUDENT ENCOUNTERS A GAP IN SEQUENTIAL COURSES?
It hasn't been as much of a problem as we thought. To the extent that we have moved away from lecture format and involved the student in the learning process, the problem of retention after a gap has been reduced. If Spanish gets put into the student in new ways, with him using the language, teaching it to peers,

and being involved as he never was in the past, it stays with him in ways it never did before. If there is a place in sequential courses where such a gap does seem to cause problems, don't schedule a gap in that spot. It took us three years to get a handle on this issue.

WILL STUDENTS BE ABLE TO EARN MORE CREDITS UNDER THE BLOCK SYSTEM?

It depends on what the school day and credits looked like before. We used to have a seven-period day. A student enrolled in six classes would earn 12 credits (six Carnegie units) a year. Taking seven classes, he could earn 14 credits (seven Carnegie units).

> **Our best students in particular now have the opportunity to take an elective impossible with our old schedule.**

Under the block system, most students are in four nine-week block classes each term. They can earn 16 credits a year (four classes each for four nine-week terms), or eight Carnegie units. By requiring students to take more credits per year, we increased enrollment in elective courses. Eliminating study halls also put more kids in class. Our best students in particular now have the opportunity to take an elective impossible with our old schedule.

WHAT ABOUT EARLY GRADUATION?

Only fairly small numbers of our graduates have gone this route. We encourage students to remain and take classes they never could fit in under our old system. This last year, students who opted to graduate a semester early came back displeased at missing the last half of their senior year with their friends. We also have an early graduation policy requiring a GPA of 3.5, 95-percent attendance, and approval of parent, principal, and counselor. If the number of early graduates is a concern, the number of students who qualify can be controlled by requirements set ahead of time.

ARE YOU COVERING AS MUCH CONTENT NOW?

I cover less, but the kids can still leave the class with more. The key is in "covering content." I do a better job now of asking what the student can do, instead of what I covered. Maybe I covered eight chapters before in my Latin class. Now students may just deal with seven, but they leave with more Latin from those seven chapters as involved learners, in groups, not just sitting while I did all the work. The Coalition of Essential Schools refers to it as "less is more," and "student as worker," and both make good sense to me now. Less content, yes—but more Latin leaves with the student.

HAS THE BLOCK SCHEDULE AFFECTED SCHOOL CLIMATE?

One reason we restructured was to reduce student/staff stress. In the past, kids ran frantically to get to classes on time—no time for chatting, for the bathroom, rush, run, knock people over. Teachers dashed from class to class in much the same way.

Now there's a calmer pace, fewer fights, less vandalism—a slowed-down pace across the building. Kids have a chance to stay and ask a question, finish that last problem, or chat with a friend, before heading to their next class—15 minutes works beautifully. Often, students from the next class come in while students from the preceding class are still around. That mix never happened before.

HOW ABOUT RESULTS?

We've documented all sorts of things, from honor roll percentages to failure rates, from daily attendance to average class size and teacher loads as well. Our results are quite positive, and we would be glad to share them with any interested group.

But our data must be considered against what is occurring in our community. Across the district, class size is increasing, money for textbooks is harder to get, state funding is tighter each year. Our school is enrolling more at-risk students and students from families below federal poverty levels. In the 1993–94 school year, our instructional calendar was reduced from 182 days to 162. One of our sister high schools has started an International Baccalaureate Program attracting some of our best students. We have shown sizable positive gains across the board, and we're even more proud of them in light of what's happening in our state and community. We'd be in a sorry state if we had not restructured—I have no proof for that, but I know it to be true.

WHAT WAS THE BIGGEST NEGATIVE FACTOR?

It's very easy to look at the block schedule as a panacea to "fix" all ills. It doesn't. We still have too many students who haven't bought into what we offer, pregnant girls, parents who don't care, teachers with oversize classes. But we have a school better in so many small ways that the end result is a much better place for the kids and for us.

WOULD YOU GO BACK TO A TRADITIONAL SEVEN-PERIOD DAY?

I don't think I could. I can't imagine having to encounter 175 kids each day and teaching five or six classes. I did it for 23 years, and it felt OK at the time—but having been on this schedule for four years, I'd never go back. I'm excited about the effect this change has had on Wasson, and I want other teachers to have a chance at the same experience—I just wish this had happened 23 years ago!

So What?

The most powerful factors in the world are clear ideas in the minds of energetic men of good will.—J. Arthur Thomson

Clear ideas in the minds of energetic men (or women) are powerful forces. For those who choose block scheduling, the issues must be not only clear, but clear and resolved, as they strive to put an idea, a mere theory, into actual practice in the school. What looks simple in theory or on paper is often extremely difficult to operationalize. Just how do schools make block scheduling work?

Naturally, the actual implementation process looks quite different at the various levels. What works at the elementary school level may be totally inappropriate at the middle or high school level. The selection of articles in section two includes two articles that focus on, respectively, the elementary level and the high school level, another that addresses all three levels, and an additional piece that sets up some guidelines that provide insight into the process itself.

Beginning with a current overview, Robert Lynn Canady and Michael D. Rettig discuss the power of innovative scheduling. While they suggest that alternative schedules may not always add hours to the school day, they feel that the *quality* of time students spend in school can be greatly improved. In their article, the authors show how well-crafted schedules can result in more effective use of time, space, and resources; improve instructional climate; and help solve instructional problems. Skill-fully presented with charted schedules for a parallel block schedule of the elementary level and two middle school block concepts, the article also suggests a number of reorganization plans suitable for high schools, including a trimester model. The ultimate vision portrayed in this inspired piece is of students "progressing from school to school in a seamless design."

In another essay by Canady, an innovative approach called "parallel block scheduling" is offered as a way to organize an elementary school. The author presents a model that permits uninterrupted small-group instruction for all students. In essence, the school day schedule is built around directed reading groups and mathematics skill groups. Using a master grid of small time segments, the schedule is shaped around these key curriculum areas.

At the high school level, perhaps the most talked about model is Carroll's "Copernican Plan." In this landmark article, Carroll proclaims that "every high school can reduce average class size, increase the number of courses or sections it offers, reduce the number of students a teacher works with each day, provide regular seminars . . . , establish an instructional environment that fosters mastery learning . . . and do all this at the present levels of funding."

A macro-scheduling plan that is by its very name revolutionizing, the Copernican Plan offers students four-hour classes for thirty days or two two-hour classes for sixty days. In the discussion, the author explains surrounding issues, such as differentiated diplomas, grades, mastery-based objectives, and individual learning plans. While the radicalness of the model may be too much, too fast for many, it is well worth reading for its intrinsic shock value in reevaluating prevailing scheduling practices at the high school level.

The article that caps off this section offers ten guidelines for implementing block scheduling that are appropriate regardless of the level of schooling. Donald G. Hackmann provides a comprehensive discussion of a collaborative approach to school reform that includes parents, students, administrators, and teachers. Through a well-articulated process, creative design and implementation of block scheduling can emerge as a highly effective alternative to traditional schooling.

Although the implementation process must be tailored to each particular situation, these four articles provide a sampling of the concerns encountered at all levels. For example, it is interesting to note the emphasis given to the high school advantages as compared to those given for the middle school or the elementary school. In any case, implementation of block scheduling brings with it a number of major implications, which leads to the next section on curriculum, instruction, assessment, and the staff development that ensures support for the changes.

The Power of Innovative Scheduling

by Robert Lynn Canady and Michael D. Rettig

Scheduling is a valuable but untapped resource for school improvement. Through our work in schools across the country, we have seen again and again how a well-crafted schedule can

- result in more effective use of time, space, and resources (human as well as material);
- improve instructional climate;
- help solve problems related to the delivery of instruction; and
- assist in establishing desired programs and instructional practices.

We believe that Deming was right when he said that it is more often the structure of an organization than the inadequacies of the people who work within it that causes problems (Bonstingl 1992). The examples we'll discuss only hint at the power of scheduling to improve schools. But, first, let's review some problems that scheduling can help alleviate.

THREE ISSUES ALL SCHOOLS FACE

Although scheduling varies from elementary school through high school, three areas of concern span all levels.

1. Providing Quality Time

Fragmented instructional time is an issue at all levels. In elementary school, a variety of practices contribute to this prob-

From *Educational Leadership*, vol. 53, no. 3, November 1993, pp. 4–10. © 1993 by the Association for Supervision and Curriculum Development. Reprinted with permission.

lem. For example, haphazardly scheduled pullout programs (for ESL or special education, for example) disrupt classroom instruction; and because the schedules of specialists (for music and art, for example) are created for periods of varying length, core teachers must plan instruction around the remaining chopped-up time. In addition, when special programs classes meet just once a week for a short period, students receive piecemeal instruction.

> **The daily schedule can have a great effect on a school's climate.**

At the middle and high school levels, fragmentation occurs in a different way. Students traveling through a six-, seven-, or eight-period day encounter the same number of pieces of unconnected curriculum each day, with little opportunity for in-depth study. In middle schools, this problem may have been exacerbated by exploratory programs, which in many schools have evolved from risk-free explorations to full academic courses with tests, grades, and homework.

Recently we worked with a district where students spent four periods daily in English, mathematics, social studies, and science, and two periods in six-week exploratory "wheels." In other words, students saw 4 core teachers and 12 exploratory teachers during the year. Is having so many teachers per day and per year consistent with what we know about middle school students?

2. Creating a School Climate

The daily schedule can have a great effect on a school's climate. At the elementary level, discipline problems can result from the way small-group reading and math instruction is scheduled. Many teachers continue to divide their classes into reading, language arts, and math groups, which meet separately with the teacher while other students complete worksheets or work in learning centers. All too often, teachers must interrupt small-group instruction to address discipline problems that arise in the back of the room.

In middle and high schools, traditional schedules create at least four situations that may contribute to the number of discipline problems.

• Many disciplinary referrals result from scheduled transitions, when large numbers of students spill into hallways, lunchrooms, and common areas, or congregate in locker rooms and bathrooms. If students are not sent to the office directly, the problems often carry over into the classroom, where teachers must deal with them before beginning instruction.

• The assembly-line, traditional period schedule contributes to the depersonalizing nature of high schools. When teachers are responsible for 100–180 students daily, and students must answer to six, seven, or eight teachers a day, it is nearly impossible to develop close relationships, which may help reduce discipline problems.

> The assembly-line, traditional period schedule contributes to the depersonalizing nature of high schools.

• Short instructional periods may also contribute to a negative classroom climate. When students who misbehave do not respond to a quick correction, many teachers send them to the office. With only 40- to 55-minute class periods, these teachers view any time taken away from classwork as unacceptable.

• The middle school schedule, in particular, often makes teaming efforts difficult. Students in seven-period schools often are enrolled in three non-core classes, while the four-teacher teams—one teacher each from English, math, science, and social studies—are assigned five classes daily. Thus, during many periods of the day, 20 percent of the students are "off core." As a result, teams must remain in a period schedule, and the team structure, which usually facilitates disciplinary control, is weakened.

3. Providing Varying Learning Time

Perhaps the most critical (and unresolved) time allocation issue that schools face is the indisputable fact that some students need more time to learn than others. In secondary schools, reliance on the Carnegie unit has made all students "Prisoners of Time" (National Education Commission on Time and Learning 1994). High schools, and to a lesser extent middle schools, experience this problem, especially in late January. After receiving their first-semester grades, some students conclude that they will not pass the subject regardless of their performance during the second semester. Believing they have nothing to gain by doing the work, some of these students act out and skip classes. In a way, we *have* created a system to handle students who need more time to learn: we give them Fs and make them repeat the course during summer school or the next academic year!

On the other end of the spectrum, possibilities for acceleration in U.S. schools are very limited. Most districts, however, offer one celebrated occasion for advancement. At the end of 7th grade in middle and junior high schools, teachers must decide whether or not a student should enroll in algebra during the 8th grade. This inflexible system forces instructors to make premature decisions about a student's potential in mathematics. If the school schedule were not as rigid, perhaps educators could make the decision to accelerate students at more appropriate times.

In elementary school, our usual reaction to the need for different amounts of time for learning is to provide individual assignments to those who learn quickly, and to regroup, slow down, and provide pull-out programs for those who need more time. The problems with these accommodations are that (1) sometimes the activities provided for those who learn quickly are thrown together haphazardly (Renzulli 1986), and (2) students placed in the lower groups fall further behind. In addition, students in pullout programs often are stigmatized by their participation in them.

SCHEDULING AS A SOLUTION
Redesigning the school schedule can help address each of these three issues. We begin with the elementary school.

Elementary School Scheduling
A number of elementary schools across the country have adopted parallel block scheduling to reduce instructional fragmentation, improve discipline, and provide regularly scheduled, yet flexible, opportunities for extended learning and enrichment (Canady 1988, 1990; Canady and Reina 1993). Figure 1 illustrates part of such a schedule, designed for four base teachers and an extension center.

Teachers A and B work with their homeroom classes for an uninterrupted 100 minutes to begin the time block shown. They can use this time for language arts and social studies or perhaps for a whole class reading lesson. Teachers A and B may team together for this block if desired.

During the next 50 minutes, Teacher A works with Reading-Writing Group 1; Teacher B instructs Group 3. Teaching about half of the class, the base teacher conducts a reading group, or a writers' workshop, or perhaps conferences with individual students. Discipline is improved because independent groups are no longer in the back of the room. The extension teacher picks up Reading-Writing Group 2 from Teacher A and Group 4 from Teacher B and escorts these student to the extension center.

> **In the extension center, students who need more time to learn receive assistance through reteaching and reinforcement.**

At the end of this 50-minute period, the extension center teacher returns Reading-Writing Groups 2 and 4 to their classrooms and picks up Groups 1 and 3 for their extension time. The rest of the school day is devoted to math, science, music, the arts, and physical education. Sleepy Hollow Elementary School in Fairfax County, Virginia, has operated a similar schedule for the past four years.

In the extension center, students who need more time to learn receive assistance through reteaching and reinforcement, and they have opportunities for practice. Any pullouts for special services—special education, English as a second language, gifted and talented, or Chapter 1—are provided during extension center time. Students who have mastered basic concepts work on enrichment activities.

The extension center position can be staffed in different ways. Increasing homeroom size frees up regular teaching staff. An alternative is to staff the center with Chapter 1, English-as-a-second-language, gifted and talented, or special education teachers. Still other options are to use the computer lab or a foreign language program as the extension center or to rotate library/media, guidance, and reading enrichment professionals for a specific period of time (three weeks, for example).

Figure 1
A Parallel Block Elementary School Schedule for
Four Base Teachers and an Extension Center

Teachers	50 mins	50 mins	50 mins	50 mins
Teacher A	Language Arts & Social Studies (Reading-Writing Groups 1 & 2)		Reading-Writing Group 1	Reading-Writing Group 2
Teacher B	Language Arts & Social Studies (Reading-Writing Groups 3 & 4)		Reading-Writing Group 3	Reading-Writing Group 4
Teacher C	Reading-Writing Group 5	Reading-Writing Group 6	Language Arts & Social Studies (Reading-Writing Groups 5 & 6)	
Teacher D	Reading-Writing Group 7	Reading-Writing Group 8	Language Arts & Social Studies (Reading-Writing Groups 7 & 8)	
Extension Center	Reading-Writing Groups 6 & 8	Reading-Writing Groups 5 & 7	Reading-Writing Groups 2 & 4	Reading-Writing Groups 1 & 3

Note: Depending on the size of the school, this plan can work with four 5th grade teachers, two 4th and two 5th grade teachers, or four teachers of four different grade levels.

Other Tips for Elementary Schools

• Schedule all specialists for equal periods of instruction on a rotating schedule during the same time block each day. Consider four- or six-day cycles, rather than the unwieldy and unfair Monday through Friday schedule.

• Rotate shared itinerant specialists who travel to different schools on a nine-week or semester basis, rather than two days a week here and two days a week there.

• Schedule recess time contiguous to another class change such as for lunch or specials' classes to reduce time lost to movement.

• Avoid short periods of time such as 15-minutes between lunch and specials. These often are wasted.

Middle School Scheduling Models
We'll look at three models at the middle school level.

The four-block schedule. One schedule being used with increasing frequency across the country greatly reduces fragmented instruction. In the four-block schedule, students spend one block of the day (about 90 minutes) in language arts, a second block in mathematics, and a third block in either social studies or science. The block of social studies/science is rotated every other day, every other unit, by semester, or on some other basis. Students spend the fourth block of the day in physical education, music, and/or exploratory courses, which meet for 90 minutes every other day. They attend only three academic courses daily.

> The four-block middle school schedule significantly reduces the daily number of class changes, thereby reducing discipline problems.

Language arts and mathematics teachers teach three groups every day for the entire year; social studies and science teachers work with three groups per day, but with six groups for the year; and physical education, exploratory, and elective teachers work with only three groups per day. With this scheduling plan, both teachers and students experience less stress and fragmentation.

The four-block middle school schedule significantly reduces the daily number of class changes, thereby reducing discipline problems. Examples of schools operating this schedule during the 1994–95 year include: Newberry Middle School in Newberry, South Carolina; Goochland Middle School in Goochland, Virginia; and Wilbur Wright Middle School in Dayton, Ohio. Districts that operate the 4 x 4 semester block high school schedule may find this plan a logical transition for middle schools.

The 75-75-30 plan (Canady and Rettig 1993). W. Marshall Sellman School in Madeira School District in Cincinnati, Ohio, implemented this unique 180-day school calendar for the 1994–95 school year. According to teachers, students, and parents, the program was a great success.

Under the Sellman plan, the school follows a fairly typical middle school team block schedule for the first 150 days. Courses end after two 75-day terms, and students begin their final six weeks of school enrolled in specialized courses, created and designed by teachers. Such specialized courses provide (1) additional learning time for students who have yet to master grade-level objectives, and (2) academically enriching activities for all students. Course titles at the Sellman School include Principles of Mathematics, Team-Accelerated Instruction, Water Science, Inventioneering, Mock Trial, and Fun with Poetry.

The concept-progress model. This approach is another attempt to address students' differing needs for learning time (Canady and Rettig 1992, Canady 1989). Several elementary and middle schools across the country are using it to provide mathematics instruction to heterogeneous groups. Figure 2 illustrates one version of this plan.

Math teachers A, B, and C present the basic concepts of a mathematical topic to their entire classes two days of every six-day cycle. Math Teacher A's Concept Math Group meets on Days 1 and 2 of the six-day cycle. During concept math time, the teacher focuses on grade-level instruction, ideally using cooperative learning, providing direct instruction, and, when needed, illustrating with manipulatives. The teacher does not test and grade students in concept groups.

After working with their whole groups, Teachers A, B, and C divide students into two Progress Math Groups—temporary, flexible, homogeneous groupings of students, based on their understanding of the basic ideas taught in the Concept Math Group. Math Teacher A instructs Progress Math Group 1 on Days 3 and 4, and Group 4 on Days 5 and 6. (Note that Progress Math Groups 1 and 4 equal Teacher A's Concept Math Group.) Teachers monitor and adjust instruction during this time, providing enrichment and additional assistance as needed; however, Progress Math Groups remain on the same topic. For example, if teachers have planned to work on long division for 18 days, Progress Math Group 2 might focus on dividing two digits into three digits, while Progress Math Group 5 might be dividing three digits into four. Note, however, that all groups work in long division for the number of days determined by the pacing guide that teachers developed at the beginning of the school

Figure 2
A Concept/Progress Middle School Model for a
Six-Day Cycle with 50- to 60-Minute Periods per Day

Teachers	1 Monday	2 Tuesday	3 Wednesday	4 Thursday	5 Friday	6 Monday
Math A	Concept Math Groups 1 & 4	Concept Math Groups 1 & 4	Progress Math Group 1	Progress Math Group 1	Progress Math Group 4	Progress Math Group 4
Math B	Progress Math Group 2	Progress Math Group 2	Concept Math Groups 2 & 5	Concept Math Groups 2 & 5	Progress Math Group 5	Progress Math Group 5
Math C	Progress Math Group 3	Progress Math Group 3	Progress Math Group 6	Progress Math Group 6	Concept Math Groups 3 & 6	Concept Math Groups 3 & 6
Computer Lab	Groups 5 & 6	Groups 5 & 6	Groups 3 & 4	Groups 3 & 4	Groups 1 & 2	Groups 1 & 2

year. Students are graded based on their progress within the topic.

In the computer lab, similar adjustments are made in the selection of the software for each group. The concept-progress model is just one way of designing the school schedule to serve students with varying instructional needs by providing

• whole-group instruction without the pressure of testing and grading;

• small groups so that teachers can monitor and adjust instruction without having to teach one group while policing another group; and

• both extended learning and enrichment time on an individual student basis.

Other Middle School Scheduling Tips

• Many middle schools can benefit from operating on some of the more popular high school block scheduling models, such as the Day 1/Day 2 schedule. Students have fewer classes daily, and fewer class changes are necessary.

• Consider adding a nontraditional core teacher to the interdisciplinary team. At Glasgow Middle School in Fairfax County, Virginia, a foreign language teacher is now on each 8th grade interdisciplinary team. At other schools, related arts teachers are on teams on a rotating basis. For example, an art teacher might be the fifth person on a team for nine weeks of art, followed by nine weeks of computer technology, nine weeks of teen living, and nine weeks of drama. Being part of the team increases the likelihood that the content of these exploratory subjects will be integrated with the core.

• Another way of reorganizing the 180-day calendar, which is similar to the 75-75-30 Plan, is the 35-(5)-35-(15)-35-(5)-35-(15) Plan. Each semester students attend regular classes for 35 days and have 5 days for reteaching and/or enrichment. Then they continue regular classes for 35 days and end the semester with 15 days for extended learning time or enrichment/electives (See Canady and Rettig 1995, Chapter 5).

High School Scheduling Models

During the past 10 years, high schools across the country have begun to implement block schedules to address curriculum fragmentation. Many schools operate alternate-day schedules, the 4 x 4 semester plan, and many variations. (For a detailed treatment of these plans see Canady and Rettig 1995). Each plan can also have a positive effect on school discipline. Here are two examples.

• *A trimester plan with daily periods for extended learning.* In the fall of 1994, Parry McCluer High School in Buena Vista, Virginia, used a trimester schedule with extended classes for enhanced learning (Canady and Rettig 1995, Chapter 4). In such a plan, students enroll in two classes per trimester; each class meets for two hours in the morning and reconvenes for an additional 45 minutes of extended learning time each afternoon. Nearly all students require this additional time for learning; however, a few have been permitted to contract out of the extended learning time for advanced study with another faculty member. An equally small number of students require more time than can be allocated each trimester to complete course objectives. If these students have worked hard and simply need more time, they may be granted an "Incomplete," which they can make up during extended learning time of the next trimester.

• *A schedule that provides algebra for all students.* In one school district—where 40 percent of the students enrolled in first-year algebra failed the course, and where approximately one-third of the students who had passed the course the previous year failed the state proficiency examination—we designed the following schedule to provide varying learning time for students in Algebra I.

As shown in Figure 3, four sections of Algebra I are scheduled in the same period or block, and the curriculum is divided into four distinct segments. During Quarter 1, all students begin together as heterogeneous groups with teachers A, B, C, and D. After completing Quarter 1, students who need more learning time are regrouped into a separate section, which repeats Part 1 with Teacher D during Quarter 2. Teachers A, B, and C continue Part 2 of the course with students who, at the time, are performing successfully. At the end of each quarter, teachers determine whether a regrouping is necessary. When a group must repeat one of the four parts of the course, we recommend using a different teaching approach—for example,

Figure 3
A Middle School Schedule That Provides Varying Learning Times for Students Taking Algebra I

Quarters	1	2	3	4	5	6	7	8
Teacher A	Part 1	Part 2	Part 3	Part 4	Students take new course. Teacher offers new course.			
Teacher B	Part 1	Part 2	Part 3	Part 4	Part 4	Computer Lab	½-credit electives available	
Teacher C	Part 1	Part 2	Part 2	Part 3	Part 3	Part 4		
Teacher D	Part 1	Part 1	Part 2	Part 2	Part 3	Part 3	Part 4	Part 4

Note: The Algebra I curriculum is divided into four parts. Quarters indicate the time it would normally take to complete ¼ of the course. In a single period or A/B schedule, this would be nine weeks. In a 4 × 4 semester plan, this would be four and a half weeks. (For more information about these scheduling plans, see Canady and Rettig 1995.)

having that teacher reteach the group using a software package in the computer lab or having one of the other four teachers reteach that part of the course.

Figure 3 shows some students finishing the course in four quarters, and some in five, six, seven, or even eight quarters. Variable learning time is provided for students, and no student is forced to sit through a repeat of the entire class. The same idea shown in Figure 3 can be designed for English, particularly for grade 9 students, by basing the parts of the course on an identified sequence of writing and reading skills.

Other High School Scheduling Tips

• Schools may periodically alter the regular schedule so that each class meets for a full day on a rotating basis. For example, in a six-period school (on a six-day cycle), teachers would meet with each of their five classes for a full day and then have a full day off for planning or professional development.

• Some schools have scheduled one long lunch period rather than two or three short periods. During this extended time the library, gym, computer lab, and outdoor recreational areas are opened for student use. Teachers schedule office hours for extra help; club meetings and other activities also may be held. Several serving sites are necessary to accommodate students purchasing lunch.

HARNESSING THE POWER OF SCHEDULING

We've looked at ways that some elementary, middle, and high schools have redesigned their schedules to reduce curriculum fragmentation, discipline problems, and student failure. We need to move beyond individual school models of scheduling, however, and toward districtwide plans. Ultimately, we envision students progressing from school to school in a seamless design. Such a plan may even enable 5th and 8th grade teachers, for example, on an every-other-year basis, to continue with their students during their first year in middle or high school.

Only in the last decade have educators begun to capitalize on the potential of scheduling to improve schools. With open minds and equal doses of creativity and technical expertise, school administrators, teachers, parents, and students can harness this power.

REFERENCES

Bonstingl, J. J. (1992). *Schools of Quality: An Introduction to Total Quality Management in Education.* Alexandria, Va.: Association for Supervision and Curriculum Development.

Canady, R. L. (October 1988). "A Cure for Fragmented School Schedules in Elementary Schools." *Educational Leadership* 46: 65–67.

Canady, R. L. (March 1989). "Design Scheduling Structures to Increase Student Learning." *Focus in Change* 1, 2: 1–2, 7–8.

Canady, R. L. (January 1990). "Parallel Block Scheduling: A Better Way to Organize a School." *Principal* 69, 3: 34–36.

Canady, R. L., and J. M. Reina. (January 1993). "Parallel Block Scheduling: An Alternative Structure." *Principal* 72, 3: 26–29.

Canady, R. L., and M. D. Rettig. (Summer 1992). "Restructuring Middle Level Schedules to Promote Equal Access." *Schools in the Middle:* 20–26.

Canady, R. L., and M. D. Rettig. (December 1993). "Unlocking the Lockstep High School Schedule." *Phi Delta Kappan:* 310–314.

Canady, R. L., and M. D. Rettig. (1995). *Block Scheduling: A Catalyst for Change in High Schools.* Princeton, N.J.: Eye On Education.

National Education Commission on Time and Learning. (1994). *Prisoners of Time: Report of the National Education Commission on Time and Learning.* Washington, D.C.: U.S. Government Printing Office.

Renzulli, J. S., ed. (1986). *Systems and Models for Developing Programs for the Gifted and Talented.* Mansfield Center, Conn.: Creative Learning Press.

Parallel Block Scheduling: A Better Way to Organize a School

by Robert Lynn Canady

I f genuine school reform is to occur, the most important changes must be made at the building level. High on the list of these changes is the redistribution of staff, space, and time within individual schools.

Most elementary schools have not changed their basic organization over the last 25 years.

Most elementary schools have not changed their basic organization over the last 25 years, even though their staffs may have doubled in that time. The classroom teacher still is randomly assigned a heterogeneous group of 25 or more students and remains responsible for them through a school day that is increasingly fragmented by students coming and going to special classes.

We feel that there is a better way to utilize teaching resources in elementary schools. It's called parallel block scheduling and it is now being used in more than 50 schools throughout the nation.

Take small group instruction in reading and mathematics, for example. At present, this usually involves sorting students into three or more groups, with each group receiving instruction while the others perform seatwork.

In parallel block scheduling, by contrast, each teacher works with two groups. While one group is receiving instruc-

From *Principal*, vol. 62, no. 3, January 1990, pp. 34–36. © 1990 by the National Association of Elementary School Principals. Reprinted with permission.

tion, the second group moves either to another classroom for support services or to an instructional area, called an extension center, for a variety of enrichment activities.

The major differences between the two organizational patterns are in the scheduling of support services and in the use of seatwork time. In the typical self-contained classroom, students may spend up to 79 percent of their time on independent seatwork activities. Support services are routinely scheduled at the convenience of resource teachers, and seldom at times that are convenient for the classroom teacher.

> Because instruction occurs continually for all students, the total amount of teacher-directed instruction is significantly increased.

With parallel block scheduling, the typical seatwork group leaves the classroom for part of a time block (usually 45 to 50 minutes) to receive supervised instruction that heretofore required small groups of students to leave their classrooms at different times during the school day. Support services for Chapter 1 and learning-disabled students are available at this time, together with such activities as speech therapy, band practice, and special classes for gifted and talented students.

For those students not in need of special instruction, the extension center—which can be located in the school cafeteria, auditorium, media center, an extra classroom, or even a hallway—offers a variety of activities to extend and enhance classroom instruction, including creative writing, computer lab, literature appreciation, independent reading, and problem solving.

During the other portion of the time block, the two groups change places. Because instruction occurs continually for all students throughout the entire time block, the total amount of teacher-directed instruction is significantly increased. Additionally, classroom teachers can teach without the disruption and fragmentation caused by students being pulled out during direct instruction periods.

Another advantage of parallel block scheduling is the reduction of the student-teacher ratio. By alternating instruction, classroom teachers are able to spend approximately half the day working with 15 or fewer students. As students receive an increased amount of teacher-directed instruction, time-on-task also increases and discipline problems are reduced.

By moving large groups simultaneously, parallel block scheduling also reduces the stigma of individual students being singled out when leaving the classroom to receive special instruction. Students in the lower reading and math groups work with the base teacher alone—without having to deal with the stressful snickers and comments of classmates in higher groups.

Grouping procedures presently used in many schools have resulted in students being resegregated during much of the school day. Parallel block scheduling allows students to spend most of the day in a mixed, heterogeneous group, but in homogeneous groups for mathematics, reading, and special education. It is therefore ideally suited for mainstreaming children from special education classes.

> **Parallel block scheduling allows students to spend most of the day in a mixed, heterogeneous group.**

Another benefit of parallel block scheduling is that additional options are available for staff assignments. In many schools, teachers welcome the opportunity to work in extension centers, where the curriculum is not tied to textbooks and system guidelines. In this environment, teachers can be highly creative in their choice of activities and instructional approaches. Teachers also welcome the opportunity to spend more time planning how they are going to teach, rather than preparing or monitoring seatwork.

Finally, studies indicate that most students, especially low achievers, appear to have increased achievement in schools that utilize parallel block scheduling.

How do you implement parallel block scheduling? A sample master schedule, built around directed reading groups (DRGs) and mathematics skill groups (MSGs), is illustrated in Figure 1. In this schedule, which breaks down a school day of six hours and 30 minutes into 39 ten-minute segments, direct reading and mathematics instruction is distributed throughout the school day in blocks that also permit students to be available for support services without being pulled out of class.

Figure 1
Sample School-Wide Parallel Block Schedule

Grades	8:30	9:30	10:30	11:30	12:25	12:30	1:30	2:30	2:30
	Homeroom Time								Dismissal Time
K		Snack	Break			Lunch	PE,M E-O-D		
1	DRGs/LA/Ext/OSS				Lunch	Sc/SS/H/possibly Art and add'l PE		MSGs/PE,M/Ext/OSS	
2/3	MSGs/PE,M/Ext/OSS		DRGs/LA/Ext/OSS		Lunch	DRGs/LA/Ext/OSS			
4/5	Sc/SS/H/possibly Art and add'l PE		MSGs/PE,M/Ext/OSS		Lunch	Sc/SS/H/possibly Art and add'l PE		DRGs/LA/Ext/OSS	

Periods: 1 2 3 4 5 6 7 8 9 10 11 12 13 14 15 16 17 18 19 20 21 22 23 24 25 26 27 28 29 30 31 32 33 34 35 36 37 38 39

(K: DRGs/LA/OSS/Ext block)

Key:

DRG	Directed Reading Group
E-O-D	Every Other Day
Ext	Extension Time
H	Health
LA	Language Arts
M	Music
MSG	Mathematics Skill Group
OSS	Other Support Services
PE	Physical Education
Sc	Science
SS	Social Studies

Figure 2
Sample Reading Placements

	Reading Levels	
	Grade 4	**Grade 5**
Basal Levels	3^1 3^2 4 4 4 5	3^2 4 5 5 5 6
Number of Students in Each DRG	12 12 14 12 13 12	10 13 12 14 12 14
Number Designation for Each DRG	1 2 3 4 5 6	7 8 9 10 11 12

Grade 4 Homeroom Assignments	Grade 5 Homeroom Assignments
Teachers	Teachers
A DRGs 1, 4	D DRGs 7, 10
B DRGs 2, 5	E DRGs 8, 11
C DRGs 3, 6	F DRGs 9, 12

After preparing a master schedule, the designated blocks should be individually developed for the various grade levels. To illustrate, let us assume that in Figure 1 the reading and language arts block for grades 4 and 5 encompasses three classes, each with a teacher and 25 students, at each grade level. The reading levels and numbers of students in each directed reading group are shown in Figure 2.

Students are assigned homeroom teachers according to reading groups, with each grade-level teacher assigned two unlike groups. Teacher A, for example, is assigned DRG 1, a low group, and DRG 4, an average group, for homeroom, reading, language arts, science, social studies, and possibly math.

As illustrated in Figure 3, when the language arts time block begins at 12:25, teacher A instructs the 14 students of DRG 4 while the 12 students in DRG 1 go to the extension center for Chapter 1 and other support services. At 1:10 the groups have five minutes to change places; the DRG 4 students go to the extension center or to a support service and the DRG 1 stu-

Figure 3
Teaching Assignments, Reading and
Language Arts Blocks

Grade 4 Teachers	Session I *12:25–1:10*	Session II *1:15–2:00*	Session III *2:05–2:50*
A	DRG 4	DRG 1	LA 1, 4
B	DRG 2	LA 2, 5	DRG 5
C	LA 3, 6	DRG 8	DRG 3
Grade 5 Teachers			
D	LA 7, 10	DRG 7	DRG 10
E	DRG 11	LA 8, 11	DRG 8
F	DRG 9	DRG 12	LA 9, 12
DRG groups available for support services and/or extension center activities.	1, 5 8, 12	3, 4 9, 10	2, 6 7, 11

dents return to their homeroom for a directed reading lesson. At 2:05, both groups are combined for additional language arts activities, such as writing, grammar, spelling, and penmanship.

A similar exchange takes place during the daily mathematics block. Regrouped according to their mathematics skills, students alternate between direct instruction and such parallel activities as computer lab, physical education, music, and library.

Parallel block scheduling requires principals and teachers to work closely in planning suitable instruction for all students. But consider the benefits of this type of scheduling, particularly for at-risk or low-achieving students:

• All students receive equal instructional time in reading and mathematics

• All students receive teacher-directed instruction unbroken by pullouts

• All students are taught in both homogeneous and heterogeneous groupings during the school day

• All students have less unsupervised seatwork activities

• All students receive increased small-group instructional time in mathematics and reading.

Restructuring schools for increased teacher-directed instruction time is critical if school reform is to result in educational improvement for all students. Parallel block scheduling is a promising way to achieve this goal.

REFERENCES

Anderson, R. C., et al. *Becoming a Nation of Readers: The Report of the Commission on Reading.* Washington, D.C.: U.S. Department of Education, 1985.

Canady, Robert Lynn. "A Cure for Fragmented Schedules in Elementary Schools." *Educational Leadership* 46 (October 1988): 65–67.

Canady, Robert Lynn and Fogliani, A. Elaine. "Cut Class Size in Half Without Hiring More Teachers." *The Executive Educator* 11 (August 1989): 22–23.

Canady, Robert Lynn and Hotchkiss, Phyllis R. "School Improvement Without Additional Cost." *Phi Delta Kappan* 66 (November 1984): 183–184.

Canady, Robert Lynn and Hotchkiss, Phyllis R. "Scheduling Practices and Policies Associated with Increased Achievement for Low Achieving Students." *Journal of Negro Education* 54 (Summer 1985): 344–355.

Canady, Robert Lynn and McCullen, Jane R. "Elementary Scheduling Practices Designed to Support Programs for Gifted Students." *Roeper Review* 7 (February 1985): 142–145.

Hotchkiss, Phyllis R. "A Comparison of Student Achievement in Reading and Mathematics in Parallel Scheduled and Surface Scheduled Schools." Ph.D. diss., University of Virginia, 1986.

Joyce, Bruce R. *Improving America's Schools.* New York: Longman, 1986.

Oakes, Jeannie. *Keeping Track: How Schools Structure Inequality.* New Haven: Yale University Press, 1985.

Sweet, Anne P. and Canady, Robert Lynn. "Scheduling for a Differentiated Reading Program." *Reading Horizons* (Fall 1979): 36–41.

The Copernican Plan to Restructure High Schools

by Joseph M. Carroll

Virtually every high school can reduce average class size; increase the number of courses or sections it offers; reduce the number of students a teacher works with each day; provide students with regular seminars on complex issues; establish an instructional environment that fosters mastery learning; get students to master more information than they learn in the seminars; and do all of this with more or less present levels of funding. How? The answer lies in what I call the Copernican Plan.

The major contribution of Nicolaus Copernicus was his explanation of the movements of the planets, which brought a new perspective to the problem: If the sun, rather than the earth, were the center of the planetary system, the movements of the planets could be explained rationally. The theory encountered great resistance. The earth as the center of the universe and God's intention that man dominate the earth had become articles of faith. The simple change in perspective proposed by Copernicus was therefore considered both incorrect and dangerous.

The Copernican Plan, likewise, tries to provide an operational perspective concerning effective instruction. It challenges some articles of educational faith and frees the American high school from the intellectual bonds of its century-old structure. Some of the major features and advantages of the plan are described here.

From *The Education Digest*, September 1990, pp. 32–35. © 1990 by The Education Digest. Reprinted with permission.

MACROSCHEDULING

The Copernican Plan is predicated on the assumption that, if the schedule for students and teachers is completely reoriented to accommodate better instructional practice, more effective instruction can be implemented. The plan proposes two alternative schedules. In the first, students enroll in *only one* four-hour class each day for 30 days. (Each student would enroll in six of these classes each year, which fulfills the required 180 school days.)

> The Copernican Plan fosters a variety of more personalized and effective instructional approaches.

In the second, students enroll in two two-hour classes for 60 days. (Each student would enroll in three of these two-course trimesters a year.) A school could schedule both 30-day and 60-day courses simultaneously, and the length of macro-classes could vary. This increased efficiency frees time in the afternoons for seminars that help students integrate knowledge across traditional disciplinary lines.

The fundamental question that the alternative schedules raise is whether, in this organization, students can actually learn as much as—or more than—they currently do. A common response is that students cannot survive a two-hour lecture, much less a four-hour one. And the prevalence of that response is a major reason why the Copernican Plan is needed. Overuse of lecturing is a major problem of high school instruction. The Copernican Plan fosters a variety of more personalized and effective instructional approaches, and it stresses adequate support for staff members to develop them.

INDIVIDUALIZED INSTRUCTION

Under the Copernican Plan, a teacher prepares for and teaches only one or two classes at a time. Furthermore, average class size can be reduced by about 20 percent. This is possible because teachers who traditionally teach five classes for the school year would teach *six* classes, thereby increasing the classes offered by 20 percent. Assuming the numbers of classes and teachers remain constant, a 20 percent reduction in class size becomes possible. In addition, with 20 percent more sections, a school has far more flexibility in grouping students. If classes now range from 10 to 25 students and average 20, under the Copernican Plan, they will range from eight to 20 and average 16.

However, the key advantage of the Copernican Plan, whatever the size of the class, is that the teacher deals with only a small number of students—and prepares for only one (or two) classes—at a time. Even with *two* two-hour classes for 60 days, a teacher's daily student load drops more than 60 percent. The time typically spent preparing for five classes can be spent planning for small groups or even for individual students within a single class. The Copernican Plan thus enables teachers to make better use of individualized instruction. Teachers can *teach students* rather than *cover classes.*

> **The key advantage of the Copernican Plan is that the teacher deals with only a small number of students at a time.**

The adoption of this type of schedule often raises reasonable questions about students' retention of what they have learned. After all, a year or more may elapse between courses in the same subject. Nevertheless, evidence indicates that retention will be as good as or better than under a traditional schedule.

DEALING WITH COMPLEX ISSUES

A major criticism of American public schools—high schools in particular—is that students are not given opportunities to deal with complex issues. Educators generally want students to deal in depth with complex problems and issues that are relevant to the subject matter they are studying and to their lives. The problem is finding enough time, especially when most complex issues are essentially interdisciplinary in nature. Considering these issues requires that students be able to read, write, understand the media, and speak effectively in discussions as either leaders or participants. And spending time to deal with such issues can mean that a teacher lacks time to cover required course content. Hence, consideration of complex issues is haphazard, tends to be shallow, and is often skewed toward a single discipline.

The Copernican Plan proposes incorporating seminars that deal with complex issues and students' special interests. Regular academic disciplines are accommodated in morning macro-classes. During most afternoons, students participate in interest/issue seminars of approximately 70 minutes and earn "I-credits." (The *I* stands for integration, as well as for interest or issues, since the purpose of these seminars is to integrate knowledge and understanding.) In seminars, students are not grouped by ability, but by interest.

I-credits are required for graduation and awarded for successful participation rather than mastery or passing examinations; students must be present and participate in the seminars. They earn more I-credits by leading a seminar and receive fewer or no credits if they fail to attend or are disruptive.

DIFFERENTIATED DIPLOMAS

The Copernican Plan proposes five diplomas: Academic Honors, Academic, Occupational Honors, Standard, and Completion. Each student's transcript identifies the diploma awarded, as well as the diplomas available. The official record, therefore, accurately reflects the accomplishments of each student. Students who wish to earn the more prestigious and demanding academic diplomas must earn additional I-credits and credits for mastery of academic material.

MASTERY-BASED CREDITS VERSUS LETTER GRADES

The Copernican Plan proposes to substitute for traditional A through F grading a system of credits that reflect[s] mastery of course objectives. The education system today is geared to teachers' covering a certain amount of material in a certain time. A student who receives an A may actually have mastered most of the material presented. Students who receive Bs, Cs, or Ds have not mastered all the material; however, they receive the same credits toward graduation as those who receive As.

In general, we assume that passing means that a student has mastered more than half of the material—usually about 60 percent for a D. The student who masters 61 percent gets a D and credit, the student who masters 59 percent gets an F and no credit. There is tremendous negative impact on the student who fails. Moreover, the assumption that the student who fails has learned nothing and is entitled to no credit is probably invalid. The current grading system simply does not account for all levels of positive achievement, and it is a major contributor to nonpromotion.

Two problems with the current grading system are the grading curve and cheating. A student who helps too many other students or unusually high perfor-mance by one or two students may "ruin the curve." Thus, there is both direct and indirect pressure on good students not to share their expertise and on poor students to cheat. Moreover, dealing with large classes makes it difficult to work directly with individual students, so teachers must rely on indirect evi-dence of performance. The Copernican Plan, with earned mas-tery credits, provides many instructional advantages, and evi-dence indicates that students should master about 25 percent more information under a mastery system.

> The current grading system simply does not account for all levels of positive achievement.

MASTERY OF COURSE OBJECTIVES

Because the schedule of the Copernican Plan allows teachers to concentrate their planning on much smaller numbers of students, teachers can assess more accurately the progress each student makes in achieving course objectives. Under the mastery-based credit system, the teacher certifies mastery. Credits are awarded as follows:

• Each student enrolls in six macroclasses in four years, for a total of 24 courses in four years. Ten mastery credits are awarded for each course. A student who masters less than 100 percent of the work receives proportionate credits.

• Students receive I-credits for the interest/issue seminars. These are awarded for attendance, participation, and attitude rather than for mastery or passing examinations.

• Physical education, health education, band, and chorus are scheduled to alternate with either the seminar or the prepa-ration/help/study period. Some music courses, such as compo-sition, can be macroclass courses. Credit for physical education and music is also based on mastery of objectives.

• Physical education, music, and other courses that cur-rently meet for a single semester or every other day for a full year can be scheduled in a variety of ways and given a value of five credits each. There is considerable flexibility in a macro-scheduled school year.

EFFICIENCY OF LEARNING

Comparing the quantity of material mastered in the Copernican high school with that mastered in the traditional high school is difficult. First, the traditional high school is neither geared to mastery nor evaluated in these terms. Under mastery learning, credit is not awarded until the specified objectives have actually been mastered.

> The Copernican Plan makes it possible to offer 20 percent more sections with the same number of teachers.

A major problem related to the efficiency of learning concerns the retention of present programs as secondary enrollments decline. Indeed, smaller high schools already have difficulty offering a full range of courses, especially foreign language and advanced-placement courses. The Copernican Plan makes it possible to offer 20 percent more sections with the same number of teachers. Thus, small high schools and schools with declining enrollments can afford to offer more specialized courses—and a better-rounded program.

INDIVIDUAL LEARNING PLANS

The Copernican Plan is also a way of providing highly individualized instruction. A high school using the plan can adapt the philosophy underlying individualized education plans as a way of encouraging management by objectives for individual students. The high school should treat students as individuals with specific interests and objectives that the school should help them achieve; it should view students as clients rather than wards. Developing an individual learning plan (ILP) for each student requires greater participation by parents and places more responsibility on students for identifying their own goals. The primary responsibility for organizing ILPs will fall on the guidance staff, but, in reality, the entire school staff will have to assist.

The use of ILPs offers a real opportunity to individualize secondary education. Students' ILPs should indicate their cur-

rent aim and the appropriate subjects and levels of mastery recommended to achieve that objective.

DEJUVENILIZING HIGH SCHOOLS

The Copernican Plan affects every aspect of the school environment—physical, organizational, and psychological—in ways
that encourage more responsible behavior on the part of
students. The schedule allows for concentration and more
mature and in-depth study of academic subjects. The mastery-
based credit system and the development of ILPs allow students
to set individual goals and to be rewarded according to their
achievement.

Field trips can be easily accommodated, and the resources
of the community can be made available in the classroom.
Students have expanded opportunities to work closely with
teachers, almost as if all teachers were coaches, and students can
follow their interests and confront important issues during the
course of the seminars. All of these features of the Copernican
Plan provide a significantly more adult, mature, productive,
personalized, relevant, and interesting high school experience
for each student.

Ten Guidelines for Implementing Block Scheduling

by Donald G. Hackmann

T hree years ago, while serving as principal of Center Middle School in Kansas City, Missouri, my faculty and I implemented a block schedule. Block-of-time schedules are becoming increasingly common in both high schools and middle schools across the country. In a nationwide survey, Cawelti (1994) found that 39 percent of high schools had fully implemented block schedules or intended to do so by 1994. In fact, all kinds of creative alternatives to traditional six- and seven-period scheduling formats are emerging—Copernican schedules with trimester macro classes (Carroll 1989), four-block semester schedules (Edwards 1993), and eight-block alternating-day schedules (Hackmann 1995), to name a few.

> **All kinds of creative alternatives to traditional six- and seven-period scheduling formats are emerging.**

In 1992, the literature on alternative scheduling configurations was not extensive and we made a few mistakes along the way. To borrow a phrase from *Getting Reform Right* (Fullan and Miles 1992), we learned that "change is a journey, not a blueprint." To help other teachers and administrators wend their way through the complexities of block scheduling, I offer the following 10 guidelines. They should encourage your faculty to adopt a collaborative approach to school reform.

From *Educational Leadership,* vol. 53, no. 3, November 1995, pp. 24–27.
© 1995 by the Association for Supervision and Curriculum Development. Reprinted with permission.

1. *Employ a systems thinking approach.* Don't implement a block schedule because it's the latest trend, but because it empowers teachers to rethink and restructure their system. Your faculty may wish to form a study group to read and discuss literature on systems thinking and educational change, such as *The Fifth Discipline* (Senge 1990) and *Change Forces* (Fullan 1993).

Discussing schoolwide issues will stimulate teachers to view reform from a systems perspective. For example, our faculty initially proposed blocks of time to minimize the number of passing periods, and thereby reduce discipline problems and improve building climate. We immediately realized, however, that 90-minute blocks would also dramatically affect teaching styles, which would in turn affect building climate in other, more substantive ways. So we began to see climate, teaching methods, and the schedule as interrelated parts of our system. We were not tinkering; we were engaging in purposeful restructuring.

> **Different schools will have different reasons for considering block scheduling.**

Different schools will have different reasons for considering block scheduling. Faculty at one Michigan high school, for example, identified three goals: (1) to permit students to enroll in one additional class each year, (2) to create larger blocks of time for instruction, and (3) to increase the time available for professional development. The common consideration: What is best for students?

Faculty in another school observed that average students tended to be invisible in the traditional schedule and needed increased teacher attention. High-achieving students, on the other hand, would generally be successful in any schedule, and low-achieving students could receive support from special programs.

2. *Secure the support of your superiors.* Restructuring may affect areas beyond your faculty's jurisdiction. For example, you may need to add or reduce staff, alter bus schedules, or deviate from negotiated contract agreements. Moreover, because block scheduling is definitely not a business-as-usual approach, you may find yourself challenging longstanding district norms. It is

therefore imperative that you first obtain tentative approval from your central office and the board of education. Frequent communication with the central office will eliminate surprises, encourage feedback, and possibly prevent you from wasting countless hours developing a schedule that will not be supported, a sure way to damage delicate staff morale.

3. *Understand the change process.* Some teachers may agree that a change is best for students, but question whether it is good for themselves. Allow teachers sufficient time to assess how they feel about the new paradigm and to prepare for it. When we first suggested block schedule, few teachers gave it serious consideration. We proceeded to address all faculty concerns, and within two months the new schedule was approved unanimously.

> **Allow teachers sufficient time to assess how they feel about the new paradigm and to prepare for it.**

It is also important to make the change when momentum peaks. If you take too much time deliberating the schedule, staff enthusiasm will start to wane. Faculty members at one high school obtained a grant to study block scheduling and spent three years researching and discussing the approach. When it came time for a vote, the rest of the staff turned the change down. The grantees had made the crucial mistake of talking the issue to death, and, in the process, plant[ed] doubts among their most avid supporters.

4. *Involve all stakeholders.* Building administrators must philosophically support any restructured schedule. Principals have three vital functions in this process: (a) to ensure that all interested parties are involved; (b) to explain the rationale for any change to the school board, central office administration, teachers, parents, and students; and (c) to actively support teachers as they struggle with the demands of changing their instructional methods.

Any changes should be teacher-driven. Teachers must have sufficient opportunity to voice concerns, and must be actively involved in developing the schedule. During the exploratory stages, it may be desirable to form a teachers' committee, keeping the entire faculty informed of the group's progress. Uninvolved, uncommitted, or indifferent teachers have no invested interest in the schedule and may be unwilling to exert the effort required to implement it successfully.

Note, too: Although you should strive for consensus, don't allow a few teachers to stall implementation. Teachers in some disciplines may believe their classes must meet every day of the year; others may simply see no need to change. You should address individual concerns, but not promise special favors to win someone's approval; you may well alienate other faculty members.

Students and parents must be involved as well; an alternative schedule may challenge their idea of the traditional school. Inform them of contemplated changes and solicit their suggestions through parent-teacher conferences, student council and PTA meetings, and school newsletters. When appropriate, invite both parents and students to participate in faculty discussions. Our middle school faculty held an informational session at our PTA open house. Parents not only offered insights the faculty had not considered, but also volunteered to write a letter of support and attend the school board meeting when the schedule was presented for approval.

> Students and parents must be involved as well; an alternative schedule may challenge their idea of the traditional school.

5. *Consult sources outside the school.* There are numerous resources you can tap to educate the faculty about scheduling alternatives. Share journal articles and videotapes; attend state and national conferences; invite educators who have implemented block schedules to come and speak candidly about any obstacles they overcame. Also visit other schools with several groups of teachers, selecting the schools carefully to provide a range of scheduling models. Make a point of inviting teachers who are skeptical of the merits of block scheduling. If they return as converts, their enthusiasm may well convert undecided staff members.

6. *Brainstorm creative alternatives.* Block scheduling allows your school to break away from the conformity of the traditional schedule. Instead of focusing on the *event* of putting a new schedule in place, play attention to *why* you need one.

Resist the temptation to simply adopt another school's model; it may be totally inappropriate for you. Your school, for example, may share staff with other buildings. Or, some of your teachers may value time each day for individual study or tutoring, whereas others may prefer a block of time for professional development.

> **Consider trying out one or more pilot schedules so that teachers and students can experience the models first-hand.**

Encourage teachers to "think outside the box," asking, "What would we like to do that our current schedule does not allow?" Write down the ideas generated, and discuss those that have merit, then explore how you can implement them. Remember, it's your program that drives the schedule, not the reverse.

You may consider trying out one or more pilot schedules so that teachers and students can experience the models first-hand. One high school staff did not want to wait until the next academic year and began experimenting with an alternating-day, six-period schedule at the start of the second semester.

7. *Examine the budgetary implications.* You may or may not need additional funding. The Coalition of Essential Schools (Sizer 1986) recommends maximum teacher loads of 80 pupils and maintains that per-pupil costs should not exceed traditional school costs by more than 10 percent. Copernican schedules (Carroll 1989), on the other hand, decrease average class size by 20 percent, but more or less maintain current funding levels.

Find the right cost-saving solutions and you may well be able to implement block schedules at no additional cost. Under our middle school's new schedule, for example, three-fourths of our faculty taught each period, while one-fourth of the staff was free to plan. This was a major departure from our previous schedule, when only one-seventh of our staff was free each period. Still, we managed to stay within the existing budget. We were not empowered to hire additional faculty, so we adjusted the schedule. We eliminated one low-enrollment elective course and increased class sizes marginally. The principal agreed to supervise in-school suspension during advisory period and also to assist cafeteria aides with cafeteria supervision. This freed up teachers who had supervised the cafeteria at lunch time to be reassigned to the classroom.

8. *Plan faculty inservices.* Address teachers' anxieties. Prepare for the "implementation dip" that will most likely occur, recognizing that things may briefly get worse before they get better (Fullan with Stiegelbauer 1991). Teachers should be encouraged to rely upon their collective expertise and to collaborate in lesson development. They can take comfort in knowing that within a few months, they will have adjusted to the instructional demands of longer periods.

> Teachers should be encouraged to rely upon their collective expertise and to collaborate in lesson development.

Encourage teachers to select the topics that they feel will be most helpful to them. For example, our middle school faculty favored the "student as worker" principle of the Coalition of Essential Schools (Sizer 1986), and so redefined our roles to be coaches and facilitators of instruction. With this paradigm shift, teachers actively engaged students in learning and gained training in methods other than straight lectures—cooperative learning, student efficacy, and student use of technology, for example.

Although teachers may express the need for extensive professional development, many agree that the best inservice is simply to jump right in. An evaluation of high schools that had implemented Copernican schedules lent credence to this position. The researchers discovered that the school with the poorest staff development program was actually the most successful at implementing the new schedule, and that, conversely, a school with extensive inservices had the poorest results (Carroll 1994). The fact is, effective teachers already teach creatively, and so should simply be encouraged to continue these innovative approaches. They should be reassured, however, that the administration will support them should they occasionally stumble and thus want to try new teaching strategies.

9. *Include an evaluation component.* You may use a variety of indicators to evaluate the schedule's effectiveness. Determine these indicators before the schedule is in place so that you can collect baseline data. Building-wide measures include student discipline referrals; attendance data; dropout rates; graduation

rates; student enrollment in upper-level courses; grade point averages; standardized test scores; honor roll data; self-esteem indicators; and feedback from surveys of teachers, parents, and students.

Some indicators may show immediate results. For example, in our initial year of implementation, we were pleased to see that discipline referrals dropped more than 60 percent, in-school and out-of-school suspensions declined proportionately, average daily attendance increased from 92 to 94 percent, and surveys confirmed that some 75 percent of the parents and students approved of the new schedule. Student achievement may take a few years to improve significantly, however. In our first year, there was a slight increase in the number of students on the honor roll, and a slight decrease in failing grades, but both gains were marginal.

10. *Share and celebrate your successes.* One unanticipated outcome of our new schedule was that faculty morale declined in the first year. One possible reason was that teachers were working long hours rewriting lesson plans and analyzing how effectively they used new teaching approaches. On the other hand, the overall building climate improved dramatically. We were so involved in the daily struggles of lesson preparation that we failed to take the time to celebrate these positive results.

Teachers can celebrate tangible successes in any number of ways: by reserving time at faculty meetings to share positive classroom experiences, by meeting in large groups to brain-storm creative teaching approaches and share effective lessons, by keeping daily or weekly journals to reflect on their professional growth, or by sharing ongoing evaluation of student progress. Finally, administrators should take advantage of every opportunity to publicly praise the faculty for their hard work, especially during the first year of implementation. All of these activities will foster a culture of collaboration and reflective practice.

REFERENCES

Carroll, J. M. (1989). *The Copernican Plan: Restructuring the American High School.* Andover, Mass.: The Regional Laboratory for Educational Improvement of the Northeast and Islands.

Carroll, J. M. (1994). "The Copernican Plan Evaluated: The Evolution of a Revolution." *Phi Delta Kappan* 76: 105–113.

Cawelti, G. (1994). *High School Restructuring: A National Study.* Arlington, Va.: Educational Research Service.

Edwards, C. M., Jr. (1995). "Virginia's 4 x 4 High Schools: High School, College, and More." *NASSP Bulletin* 79, 571: 23–41.

Fullan, M. (1993). *Change Forces: Probing the Depths of Educational Reform.* London: The Falmer Press.

Fullan, M. G., with S. Stiegelbauer. (1991). *The New Meaning of Educational Change,* 2nd ed. New York: Teachers College Press.

Fullan, M. G., and M. B. Miles. (1992). "Getting Reform Right: What Works and What Doesn't." *Phi Delta Kappan* 73: 744–752.

Hackmann, D. G. (1995). "Improving the Middle School Climate: Alternating-Day Block Schedule." *Schools in the Middle* 5, 1: 28–34.

Senge, P. M. (1990). *The Fifth Discipline: The Art and Practice of the Learning Organization.* New York: Doubleday.

Sizer, T. R. (1986). "Rebuilding: First Steps by the Coalition of Essential Schools." *Phi Delta Kappan* 68: 38–42.

Now What?

Ideas shape the course of history.—John Maynard Keynes

Now what? With block scheduling in place as a scheduling alternative, what are the implications for teaching? How does block scheduling impact on the actual programs? How does curriculum, instruction, and assessment change? What are the emergent needs of staff, and how does the schedule provide time for teachers to learn, too?

To address these questions, two articles appear in this section. One discusses how the instructional program is affected by block scheduling; the other outlines a plan for providing professional development time directly in the planning of the block scheduling. Both elements are essential in the move toward block scheduling.

Robin Fogarty provides an encompassing look at how block scheduling dictates instructional strategies and curricular frameworks that may differ from the traditional approaches. "Block Scheduling: It's Not a Question of Time" addresses the underlying rationale for block scheduling—that is, schooling designed with the learners' needs at the center. The article surveys specific instructional methodologies (cooperative learning, higher-order thinking, multiple intelligences, graphic organizers), as well as various curricular frameworks (projects, themes, performances, problem-based learning, service learning, case studies) that naturally follow from a move to larger blocks of time to teach and learn. In addition, a tri-assessment model is introduced to provide a balanced assessment plan compatible with these teaching designs. The need for a shift to these more holistic models of learning is discussed in this article, and the stage is clearly set for more learner-centered schooling.

Naturally, the shift to more complex models of instruction and curriculum dictates the need for well-articulated professional development. In a timely article, Brenda Tanner, Robert L. Canady, and Michael D. Rettig outline models of scheduling that create blocks of time for both students and teachers to be involved in study and learning. The discussion focuses on scheduling time to maximize staff development opportunities without sacrificing time for students to learn. While the secondary school is targeted, the models are quite adaptable to other levels of schooling.

Block Scheduling: It's Not a Question of Time

by Robin Fogarty

LOCK SCHEDULING DEFINED

"I'm concerned about block scheduling. I teach English literature, and I don't know how I'm going to use ninety minutes. I
don't have a lab set-up like they have in science or computers. So
what am I going to do with the students for an hour and a half?
They can only read so much, and I can only talk for so long."

As an educational consultant, I replied, "It's not a question of
time. It's a question of learning." I went on to tell the teacher
about the use of active-learning strategies, strategies that help
students construct meaning and make sense of learning. I
showed her several ideas from cooperative learning and suggested small-group work with graphic organizers. I told her that
students can "map" their perception of a story, or they can
compare two characters using Venn diagrams. We talked about
using themes and studying entire genres rather than singling
out one topic. In addition, I told her about the possibility of doing units in conjunction with other disciplines.

Our brainstorming led to the idea of using multiple intelligences to ensure multidimensional learning. As I punctuated
the discussion with specific suggestions, the English teacher
joined in with additional ideas. Her body relaxed and her face
lightened as she began to see the opportunities for energized
learning.

From *Think About . . . Block Scheduling.* © 1995 by IRI/Skylight Training and
Publishing, Inc. Reprinted with permission.

Figure 1
Bell Schedule (Traditional)

Time	Period	Subject*
8:30 – 9:15	1	Homeroom/Advisory
9:15 – 10:00	2	English
10:00 – 10:45	3	Math
10:45 –11:30	4	PE
11:30 –12:15	5	History
12:15 –12:45	6	Lunch
12:45 – 1:30	7	Keyboarding
1:30 – 2:15	8	Biology
2:15 – 3:00	9	Exploratory (Art, Band)
		*Varies according to grade level, electives, and track.

At first glance, this teacher's concerns seem grounded in a dilemma specific to her discipline, but they are relevant to other disciplines as well. Primarily, these concerns are (1) What do we do with block scheduling? and (2) How does our teaching change?

There are two models pertinent to finding the answers to these questions: the *bell schedule* and the *block schedule*. The bell schedule refers to the traditional mailbox-slot design of departmentalized junior high and high schools in which the bell rings every 43–50 minutes to signal student rotation to the next class (fig. 1). Typically, bell schedules range from seven-period to ten-period designs. Naturally, the more periods there are, the shorter the time frames for each slot.

The block schedule is an alternative to what Goodlad (1984) calls the "subject matter slices." Block scheduling, according to Beane (1990), is "the everyday schedule formed around the activity, problems or projects that young people are involved with" (p. 94). Block scheduling may be implemented for a semester or a year. "Team blocks" are scheduled around "whole school" times, allowing the predetermined block schedule to account for the hub of schoolwide activities. Team blocks may be quite flexible. Determined by the teachers and students and based on myriad concerns—length of unit, activities planned, needed resources, and staffing possibilities—block, flexible, or modular (Merenbloom 1992) schedules often change as needed.

Current literature is replete with references to block scheduling models. Sizer (1984) and Goodlad (1984) first allude to changing schedules into larger blocks of time. Goodlad delineates ideas about schools within a school, teams of teachers, clusters of kids, and chunks of time to plan. He describes the docile thinkers, passive learners, and bored students who need to be intensely involved in their own learning. Vars (1993) suggests blocks of time for problem-solving activities. Merenbloom (1992) refers to block or modular schedules, stressing common planning time for teacher teams and for teaching designs. The modules are blocks that are subdivided as needed. Schrenko (1994) provides a lengthy discussion, with a variety of examples, about flexible block time and learner-centered scheduling.

> Current literature is replete with references to block scheduling models.

The 4:4 block plan offers several examples, which are illustrated in figures 2–6. The generic block schedule (fig. 2) shows a typical assortment of classes for one semester, while figures 3–6 illustrate full four-year programs for advanced placements (fig. 3), advanced studies (fig. 4), technical/vocational studies (fig. 5), and technical/vocational studies (nonclassified) (fig. 6). With the four-block day, the schedule for teachers is also impacted, as seen in figure 7. Overall, with this model, teachers have longer class periods, but they also have more planning time, fewer teaching periods, and fewer total students.

The Copernican Plan (Carroll 1992) is a revolutionary version of block scheduling for high schools that has received much attention. Briefly, the Copernican Plan "deploys staff and students to allow for more effective teaching" (Schrenko 1994,

Figure 2
Block Scheduling

	Monday	Tuesday	Wednesday	Thursday	Friday
BLOCK I	English 10	Geometry	English 10	Geometry	English 10 Geometry
BLOCK II	French III	Biology	French III	Biology	French III Biology
BLOCK III	Computer Concepts	Computer Concepts	Computer Concepts	Computer Concepts	Computer Concepts
BLOCK IV	PE 10	Fine Art II	PE 10	Fine Art II	PE 10 Fine Art II

Figure 3
Advanced (Advanced Placement) Studies
A 23-Credit Diploma
(90-Day Courses and Four-Period Day)

Grade 9	Grade 10	Grade 11	Grade 12
1st Session (90 Days)			
English 9	English 10	English 11	English 12
Earth Science	Geometry	AP US Hist Prep	AP Lang Prep
PE/Health 1	Chemistry	Language 1	AP Calculus Prep
Band or Elective	Band or Elective	AP Biology	Physics
2nd Session (90 Days)			
World History	PE/Health 2	PreCalculus	AP English 12*
Biology 1	Adv Math/Trig	AP US History*	AP Language*
Algebra 2	Adv Chemistry	Language 2	AP Calculus*
Band or Elective	Band or Elective	AP Biology*	US Government

* AP are Advanced Placement college level courses

Figure 4
Advanced (Community College) Studies
A 23-Credit Diploma
(90-Day Courses and Four-Period Day)

Grade 9	Grade 10	Grade 11	Grade 12
1st Session (90 Days)			
English 9	English 10	English 11	AP English 12 Prep
Earth Science	Geometry	US History	Western Civ I*
PE/Health 1	Chemistry	Gen Biology I*	Calculus I*
Language 1	Language 3	Software Intro*	Physics
2nd Session (90 Days)			
World History	PE/Health 2	PreCalculus	AP English 12*
Biology 1	Adv Math/Trig	CIS Intro*	Western Civ II*
Algebra 2	Biology 2	Gen Biology II*	Calculus II*
Language 2	Language 4	Economics*	US Government

*3-semester-hour community college course

Figure 5
Technical/Vocational Studies
A 21-Credit Diploma
(90-Day Courses and Four-Period Day)

Grade 9	Grade 10	Grade 11	Grade 12
1st Session (90 Days)			
English 9	English 10	English 11	English 12
Earth Science	Algebra 2	Band or Elective	Band or T/C Elective
Careers	Biology	Path Elective	Tech/College Elective
Band or Elective	Band or Elective	Path Elective	Tech/College Elective
2nd Session (90 Days)			
World Geography	PE/Health 2	US History	US Government
PE/Health 1	Informal Geometry	Band or Elective	Band or T/C Elective
Algebra 1	Chemistry	Path Elective	Tech/College Elective
Band or Elective	Band or Elective	Path Elective	Tech/College Elective

Figure 6
Technical/Vocational Studies
Non-Classified Student
(90-Day Courses and Four-Period Day)

Grade 9	Grade 10	Grade 11	Grade 12
1st Session (90 Days)			
Reading Workshop	English 10	English 11	English 12
Writing Workshop	Algebra 2	Informal Geometry	Path Elective
Math Workshop	Health/Drs. Ed	Path Elective	Path Elective
PE 1	Path Elective	Path Elective	Path Elective
2nd Session (90 Days)			
English 9	PE/Health 2	US History	US Government
Earth Science	Biology 1	Path Elective	Path Elective
Algebra 1	World Geography	Path Elective	Path Elective
Careers	Path Elective	Path Elective	Path Elective

Figure 7
The High School Teacher's Day

	Period Length	Teaching Periods	Class Time	Planning	Students Class	Total
Six-Period Day	50 min.	5	4.2 hrs.	0.8 hrs.	25	125
Four-Period Day	90 min.	3	4.5 hrs.	1.5 hrs.	25	75

33). However, Carroll clearly states that the "Copernican Plan is not about block scheduling. It is about the relationship between time and learning" (Carroll 1994, 26).

Students may take two, three, or four classes, with blocks ranging from a modified Copernican Plan of 70 to 90 minutes to a true Copernican model of macroclasses that meet for 226 minutes for 30 days, 100 minutes for 60 days, or 90 minutes for 45 days. As radical as it may sound, the Copernican Plan may be a model worth exploring as schools investigate alternatives to the traditional bell schedule (fig. 8).

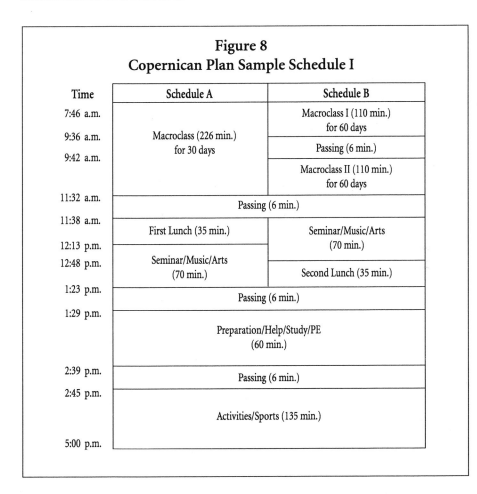

Figure 8
Copernican Plan Sample Schedule I

Time	Schedule A	Schedule B
7:46 a.m.		Macroclass I (110 min.) for 60 days
9:36 a.m.	Macroclass (226 min.) for 30 days	
9:42 a.m.		Passing (6 min.)
		Macroclass II (110 min.) for 60 days
11:32 a.m.	Passing (6 min.)	
11:38 a.m.	First Lunch (35 min.)	Seminar/Music/Arts (70 min.)
12:13 p.m.		
12:48 p.m.	Seminar/Music/Arts (70 min.)	Second Lunch (35 min.)
1:23 p.m.	Passing (6 min.)	
1:29 p.m.	Preparation/Help/Study/PE (60 min.)	
2:39 p.m.	Passing (6 min.)	
2:45 p.m.	Activities/Sports (135 min.)	
5:00 p.m.		

INSTRUCTIONAL STRATEGIES

As schools move toward a learner-centered approach and integrated, holistic learning that connects ideas purposefully, they recognize the need for large blocks of time. Paradoxically, when teachers get these blocks, they are not always sure how to orchestrate their teaching for the new time allotments.

Perhaps the answers lie within two realms: *instructional strategies* and *curricular frameworks*. The instructional strategies that seem most appropriate for the learner-centered approach to block scheduling include the *cooperative learning* structure that ensures active learning, the incorporation of *graphic organizers* as tools for small group interactions, the *multiple intelligences* approach that taps the full range of human potential, and

Figure 9
Instructional Strategies for Block Scheduling

Cooperative Learning	Higher-Order Thinking	Multiple Intelligences	Graphic Organizers
1. Rhetorical Question	1. Compare	1. Verbal/Linguistic	1. Webbing
2. Direct Question	2. Classify	2. Visual/Spatial	2. Mapping
3. Turn to Your Partner and . . .	3. Prioritize	3. Mathematical/ Logical	3. Venn Diagrams
4. Think/Pair/ Share	4. Evaluate	4. Musical/ Rhythmic	4. Matrices
5. Triads	5. Cause/Effect	5. Bodily/ Kinesthetic	5. Fishbones
6. Dyads	6. Sequence	6. Interpersonal/ Social	6. Flow Charts
7. 2-4-8 Interview	7. Hypothesize	7. Intrapersonal/ Introspective	7. Priority Ladders
8. Traveling Cluster	8. Generalize		8. Agree/Disagree
9. Cooperative Learning	9. Infer		9. Cause/Effect Circles
10. Jigsaw	10. Predict		10. 5 W Words
11. Wrap Around	11. Brainstorm		11. Right Angles
12. Human Graph	12. Personify		12. Pie Charts

the focus on *higher-order thinking* that promotes rigor and challenge in student problem solving (fig. 9).

Cooperative Learning

Cooperative learning strategies provide viable methods for the
interactive classroom, but they require a shift from formal to
informal, small groups to large groups, and lecture to guidance.
Cooperative learning means individual involvement with roles
and responsibilities, as well as teamwork and attention to group
goals. Imagine triads working on building a model of the human cell to demonstrate their understanding in biology class or
partners predicting their interview questions. Cooperative

learning shepherds the interaction toward increased student ownership. In addition, cooperative learning provides a platform for learning about the social skills and social graces that are intrinsically related to the overall success of our students.

Graphic Organizers

Teamwork requires clear guidelines and student accountability. Graphic organizers such as analysis webs, mind maps, and Venn diagrams serve as motivating, visible, and productive tools.

Using large newsprint and markers, students could gather information from a film on the circulatory system or create a prediction chart prior to a lecture on the causes of the Depression. Not only do the graphics foster reflective thinking and careful articulation among team members, they also provide visible evidence of thinking and accountability for the completion of the task.

> By embracing the multiple intelligences theory, educators capture the heart and soul of learners.

Multiple Intelligences

Immersion in an experiment on chemical bonding, journaling in the math class on problem-solving strategies, oral and written reports on how to stop the hiccups, the use of logic to argue a point about justice, and the patterns of memorable lyrics in songs are the sum and part of every classroom. By embracing the multiple intelligences theory, educators capture the heart and soul of learners. Specifically, Gardner's theory of multiple intelligences recognizes seven different realms of knowing, learning, and assessing: bodily, intrapersonal, visual, interpersonal, verbal, mathematical, and musical (Gardner 1983). Block scheduling permits, and, in fact, promotes this kind of multidimensional learning.

Higher-Order Thinking

Learning that challenges student thinking, that requires students to not only gather information but also to analyze that data and synthesize it for meaningful application, is an ideal model of instruction for block scheduling. Students have time to think, problem solve, and make decisions. They have ample opportunity to work diligently at a task, get stuck, work through the struggle, and get "unstuck." They have the time to think creatively and critically. Infusing higher-order thinking into the block-scheduled classes sparks instruction with the rigor and vigor necessary for students to make sense of the world and construct meaning in their minds. For example, students could conduct a courtroom simulation using the skills of a thoughtful classroom—predicting, hypothesizing, rationalizing, and justifying.

CURRICULAR FRAMEWORKS

Complementing the instructional focus on learner-centered strategies is the focus on curricular frameworks for relevant, purposeful learning. Included in the curricular frameworks that promote meaningful learning are *project-oriented curriculums* that rally instructional activities, *thematic units* that create umbrellas to learning, *performance-based learning* that culminates in a high-profile finale, *service learning* that adapts a community focus to purposeful projects, *problem-based learning* that induces solutions to real-life problems, and *case studies* that ground learning in the analysis of complex situations and the immersion of debriefing sessions (fig. 10).

Projects

Block scheduling that fosters the use of in-depth projects and project-oriented learning is a viable way to integrate curriculums. As students create a brochure about their community, plan a spaghetti dinner fundraiser, or orchestrate the actual building of a house, they integrate multidimensional skills, talents, and information that require large chunks of time. Teams of teachers and students, planning and working together, become the norm when time permits this kind of purposeful learning. Tasks are relevant, the product is visible, and the instruction *is* the assessment.

Thematic Units

Integrated thematic instruction creates an organizing center for curriculum development that is visible and exciting to students. Themes such as fashion, origins, and habits ignite learning and provide a platform for a fresh view of a curriculum tailored to

Figure 10
Curricular Frameworks

Projects	Themes	Performances	Problem-Based Learning	Service Learning	Case Studies
Newspaper	Topic: Habits	Persuasive Speech	Gangs	Recycling	Opening Small Business
Brochure	Concept: Patterns	Lab Experiment	Polluted River	Playground	Abortion
Invention	Event: Field Trip	Simulation	Violence in Schools	Graffiti	Smoking
Art Exhibit	Project: "Rube Goldberg" Invention	Role Play	Handicapped	Design a School	Locker Search
Puppet	Novel: *Jurassic Park*	Demonstration	Geriatrics	Nursing Home	Brochures
Student-Made Book	Song: "Scarborough Fair"	Gymnastics	Welfare	Parks	Justice
Diorama	Problem: Pollution	Athletics	Homeless	Arts	1st Amendment (Free Speech)
Collection	Film: *Hoop Dreams*	Musicals	Safety	Elections	2nd Amendment (Firearms)
Sculpture		Recitals	Day Care	Drug Education	Courage
Poster		Auditions	Racism		Mercy Killing
Mural		Dance	Women's Equity		
Mosaic		Fashion Show	Drugs		
Creation Museum		Videotaping			

block scheduling. Themes emerge from topics, concepts, events, projects, novels, songs, and problems; they can last two weeks or two months. Themes are magnets that draw multiple disciplines into the theme center; they are fun, energizing, and provide inspiration for more connected and brain-compatible learning.

> Performances pull together myriad aspects of student learning into meaningful and relevant purposes.

Performance-Based Learning

Just as projects provide a curricular framework for integrated learning that requires chunks of time, performance-based learning dictates alternative scheduling. You don't produce a musical in forty-three-minute work sessions. More likely, you design the set, print the program, and struggle through a dress rehearsal within various blocks of time—time that easily spills over the traditional bell schedule. Performances pull together myriad aspects of student learning into meaningful and relevant purposes.

Problem-Based Learning

Problem-based learning begins with the identification and agreement of the problem base. Often the process begins with a "muddle" or dilemma, and the problem focus is eventually sifted from the confusion. For example, students may be aware of community concerns, such as gang activity or the homeless. From there, they begin to narrow their focus to a manageable chunk. Or, a problem may be framed for the students, such as the task of engineering a model bridge that meets certain weight-bearing requirements. They can also attack a more open-ended problem, such as considering ergonomics while designing office furniture. Problem-based learning may also sprout from a school focus. One class accepted the challenge of planning a community effort playground for their school, while another group worked to design a high school of the future.

Service Learning

Service learning is a subset of problem-based learning. It has a particular civic focus that is stressed in current educational literature. Service learning calls on the skills, talents, and efforts of the students in partnership with a community goal. In essence, students provide services for the project and, in turn, learn in many ways. Service learning presents a viable model for integrated learning and is well suited to the block-scheduling model. Service learning is targeted to a specific, visible, and worthy cause that beckons the resourcefulness of the community youth. One example is a Native American project in New Mexico in which students joined the community to search for "solutions to pollution" in the river that runs through their land. It takes time to develop, which block scheduling supports.

> Case studies motivate youngsters with inviting, intriguing, and relevant dilemmas.

Case Studies

Grounded in the genre of integrated models of curriculum and instruction is the case study model. Based on an elaborate scenario, or case, students are engaged in an investigation. Just as a case study in medical research delineates a particular illness complete with a patient profile of symptoms, related behaviors, procedures, treatment, and results, case studies in the classroom provide a telescopic frame for exploring, investigating, and generalizing. Using a specific scenario, students dissect the case in an effort to prove a point, draw a conclusion, or justify their reasoning. The open-endedness of classroom case studies promotes creative as well as critical thinking. The inductive model provides fertile ground for observation, attention to detail, inference, problem solving, and character training in moral decision making. Case studies motivate youngsters with inviting, intriguing, and relevant dilemmas, which require plenty of time to think, analyze, and reason.

THE TRI-ASSESSMENT MODEL

Assessment needs to be considered when planning for block scheduling. A balanced assessment model is best suited to the learner-centered approach (fig. 11). *Traditional assessment* often focuses on grades, grade-point averages, and rankings. Included in traditional assessments are classwork, homework, and criterion-referenced and standardized measures. *Portfolio assess-*

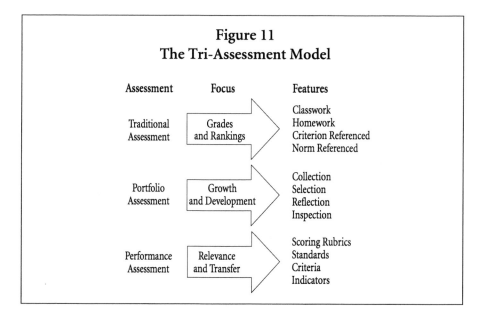

Figure 11
The Tri-Assessment Model

Assessment	Focus	Features
Traditional Assessment	Grades and Rankings	Classwork Homework Criterion Referenced Norm Referenced
Portfolio Assessment	Growth and Development	Collection Selection Reflection Inspection
Performance Assessment	Relevance and Transfer	Scoring Rubrics Standards Criteria Indicators

ment, on the other hand, tends to focus on the growth and development of student potential. Phases of the portfolio development process include collecting and selecting items, reflecting on the significance of the items as indicators of growth, and inspecting the portfolio for signs of progress. *Performance assessment* focuses on the direct observation of a student's performance. Procedures for using performance assessment effectively include developing scoring rubrics and using predetermined standards, criteria, and indicators.

The issue of block scheduling is complex. It requires a belief in the need for a more learner-centered approach to school and an understanding of the domino effect on schooling that is inherent in block scheduling. It requires flexibility for change, and it calls for partnerships with all sectors of the school community. Nonetheless, the benefits of reduced class size, increased numbers of courses or sections, reduced student load per teacher (Carroll 1990), cost effectiveness, increased student achievement (Shore 1995), and a better school climate (Schoenstein 1995) are worth the struggle it takes to shift to blocks. After all, block scheduling is not a question of time, it's a question of learning.

REFERENCES

Beane, J. A. 1990. *A middle school curriculum: From rhetoric to reality.* 2d ed. Columbus, Ohio: National Middle School Association.

Bellanca, J. 1990. *The cooperative think tank: Graphic organizers to teach thinking in the cooperative classroom.* Palatine, Ill.: IRI/Skylight Publishing.

————. 1992. *The cooperative think tank II: Graphic organizers to teach thinking in the cooperative classroom.* Palatine, Ill.: IRI/Skylight Publishing.

Burke, K. 1994. *The mindful school: How to assess authentic learning.* Palatine, Ill.: IRI/Skylight Publishing.

Burke, K., R. Fogarty, and S. Belgrad. 1994. *The mindful school: The portfolio connection.* Palatine, Ill.: IRI/Skylight Publishing.

Carroll, J. 1989. *The Copernican plan: Restructuring the American high school.* Andover, Mass.: Regional Lab for Educational Improvement—NE and Islands.

————. 1990. The Copernican plan to restructure high schools. *Education Digest,* September.

————. 1992. *The Copernican plan evaluated: The evolution of a revolution.* Andover, Mass.: Regional Lab for Educational Improvement—NE and Islands.

————. 1994. Organizing time to support learning. *The School Administrator,* March.

Edwards, C., Jr. 1993. The four period day: Restructuring to improve student achievement. *NASSP Bulletin,* May.

Fogarty, R. 1990. *Designs for cooperative interactions.* Palatine, Ill.: IRI/Skylight Publishing.

————. 1991. *The mindful school: How to integrate the curricula.* Palatine, Ill.: IRI/Skylight Publishing.

Fogarty, R., and J. Bellanca. 1986. *Teach them thinking: A handbook of classroom strategies.* Palatine, Ill.: IRI/Skylight Publishing.

Fogarty, R., and J. Bellanca, eds. 1995. *Multiple intelligences: A collection.* Palatine, Ill.: IRI/Skylight Publishing.

Fogarty, R., and J. Stoehr. 1995. *Integrating curricula with multiple intelligences: Teams, themes, and threads.* Palatine, Ill.: IRI/Skylight Publishing.

Gardner, H. 1983. *Frames of mind.* New York: Basic Books.

Goodlad, J. I. 1984. *A place called school: Prospects for the future.* New York: McGraw-Hill.

Kovalik, S., with Karen Olsen. 1993. *ITI: The model in Integrated Thematic Instruction*. Arizona: Susan Kovalik and Associates.

Loundsbury, J. H., ed. 1992. *Connecting the curriculum through interdisciplinary instruction*. Columbus, Ohio: National Middle School Association.

Merenbloom, E. Y. 1992. *The team process: A handbook for teachers*. 3rd and enlarged ed. Columbus, Ohio: National Middle School Association.

Newberg, N. A. 1995. Clusters: Organizational patterns for caring. *Phi Delta Kappan*, May.

Noddings, N. 1992. *The challenge to care*. New York: Teacher's College Press.

Pegis, J. M., ed. 1993. *Getting it all together: Curriculum integration in the transition years*. Ontario: The Metropolitan Toronto School Board.

Scearce, C. 1992. *100 ways to build teams*. Palatine, Ill.: IRI/Skylight Publishing.

Schoenstein, R. 1995. Making block scheduling work. *The Education Digest*, February. Condensed from *Virginia Journal of Education* 88 (1994): 6–12.

Schrenko, L. 1994. *Structuring a learner-centered school*. Palatine, Ill.: IRI/Skylight Publishing.

Shore, R. 1995. How one high school improved school climate. *Educational Leadership*, 76–78.

Sizer, T. 1984. *Horace's compromise: The dilemma of the American high school*. Boston, Mass.: Houghton-Mifflin.

Vars, G. F. 1993. *Interdisciplinary teaching: Why and how?* Columbus, Ohio: National Middle School Association.

Williams, B. 1993. *More than 50 ways to build team consensus*. Palatine, Ill.: IRI/Skylight Publishing.

Scheduling Time to Maximize Staff Development Opportunities

by Brenda Tanner, Robert L. Canady, and Michael D. Rettig

T he current trend to block scheduling in high schools has become a catalyst for instructional change. A major concern for many teachers in schools which are implementing block scheduling is the design of lessons appropriate for the 80- to 120-minute class periods. It is becoming increasingly important, therefore, to provide staff development to support this aspect of the high school restructuring movement. Ironically, the change to block scheduling that has generated a need for new teaching strategies can also provide extended time *during the school day* for staff development.

> Block scheduling can also provide extended time *during the school day* for staff development.

We begin by examining the need to provide professional development time for teachers during regular school hours without sending the students home. Next, we offer three high school schedules that were designed to create extended learning time for both teachers and students. In the first plan, the 180-day school year is reconfigured to provide between two and 15 days for extended instructional activities and staff development. In the second plan, class periods are combined within the school day to create large blocks of time. In the third plan, we show how a school using a 4/4 semester schedule, where students complete four classes each semester, can provide a full, duty-free day every 20 school days for teacher planning.

From *Journal of Staff Development*, vol. 16, no. 4, Fall 1995, pp. 14–19. © 1995 by the National Staff Development Council, P.O. Box 240, Oxford, Ohio 45056, (513) 523-6029. Reprinted with permission.

TIME FOR LEARNING

If we view schools as learning organizations, educators must develop schedules that are supportive of the learning process for both students and teachers. Over the past few years, secondary schools have begun to explore alternatives to the standard 40- to 55-minute class period and the six, seven, or eight period daily schedule in order to enhance student learning (Canady & Rettig, 1995). As the National Commission on Time and Learning (1994) noted, "[It] is myth that schools can be transformed without giving teachers the time they need to re-tool themselves and reorganize their work" (p. 8).

> Instructional time is sometimes forfeited for the sake of staff development—a politically unpopular sacrifice.

Even though new programs create a need for staff development, little attention has been given to creating time for teachers to study and learn. Joyce and Showers (1988) discuss the problem of "arranging time for study groups and coaching teams" in the school "workplace."

> The workplace was organized long before anyone anticipated that life-long study and the careful preparation of learning environments would be necessary . . . Now we have to face the problem of arranging time for study groups and coaching teams to operate effectively. (p. 145)

Traditionally, educators have attempted to provide time for staff development and curriculum revision by scheduling short workshops or committee meetings before and after school, by compacting a year's worth of activity into a handful of teacher workdays prior to the arrival of students in the fall, and by sending students home during the school year either for whole or half-days.

Each of these models has well-known problems, one of which is that instructional time is sometimes forfeited for the sake of staff development—a politically unpopular sacrifice. In the report *Prisoners of Time,* the National Commission on Time and Learning (1994) recognized an urgent need for professional development time and cautioned against taking staff development time from instructional time.

> The last thing districts should encourage is sending children home to provide time for "teacher professional days." We will never have truly effective schools while teachers' needs are met at the expense of students' learning time. (p. 36)

We suggest a relatively new concept: embedding extended periods of staff development time into the regular workday, without sacrificing instruction for students. First, we provide a plan which provides two, three, five, 10 or even 20 full days each school year when groups of teachers have no instructional responsibilities. Next, we show how single-period and 4/4 semester block schedules can be modified temporarily to provide extended periods of planning or staff development time for teachers on a rotating basis.

The real issue is not lack of time, but efficient use of the time that already exists.

SCHEDULING STAFF DEVELOPMENT DAYS WITHOUT SENDING STUDENTS HOME

If administrators are willing to explore new possibilities in scheduling, they might find that the real issue is not lack of time, but efficient use of the time that already exists (Loucks-Horsley et al., 1987). Thinking of time only in terms of quarters, semesters, or years limits flexibility in designing schedules. However, if available time is seen as 180 discrete units which can be grouped according to need, the possibilities are increased for developing a multitude of plans (Canady, 1994).

Figure 1 illustrates how a standard 180-day school year can be modified to provide four terms of instruction rather than two semesters. With this schedule, teachers provide the core of instruction during the 80-day fall and spring terms. At the end of each term, 10 days are provided for a host of activities for both students and teachers. For example, this 10-day period could provide additional learning time for students who have not yet mastered certain concepts, while giving other students

Figure 1
Two Terms Throughout the School Year with
Daily Blocks (The 80(10) - 80(10) Plan)

Terms Through-out the Year / Daily Schedule	1 Fall Term 80 Days	2 Midsession 10 Days	3 Spring Term 80 Days	4 Final Session 10 Days
Block I 112 minutes	Course 1	Elective, Community Service, Remedial Work, etc.	Course 5	Elective, Community Service, Remedial Work, etc.
Block II 112 minutes	Course 2	**Staff Dev. for selected teachers**	Course 6	**Staff Dev. for selected teachers**
Period 5 48 minutes + 24 min. lunch	Course 3 and Lunch	Course 3 and Lunch	Course 3 and Lunch	Course 3 and Lunch
Block III 112 minutes	Course 4	Elective and Study	Course 7	Elective and Study

Note: Blocks I, II, and III are the equivalent of two class periods of 56 minutes each. This plan also can be used with a single period schedule for a six-, seven-, or eight-period day.

time to extend their learning through special projects, elective studies, and internships.

In addition to providing extra time for student learning, the 80(10)-80(10) plan outlined in Figure 1 can be used to develop blocks of time for teacher study and planning. Utilizing such a schedule, high schools can rotate teacher assignments during the two 10-day sessions (terms 2 and 4) to free a portion of the teachers from teaching responsibilities or assigned duties.

To illustrate how this plan would work, think of a 1,000-student high school with a 60-teacher faculty, each teaching five of seven periods. For the purpose of staff development, think of the schedule in terms of a two-year cycle with each year containing two 10-day sessions in which to provide time for teachers to participate in non-teaching activities such as curriculum planning, observation of peers, or other professional growth opportunities.

Working with universities or other providers, schools could offer mini-courses on topics such as cooperative learning, Paideia seminar teaching (Adler & Van Doren, 1984), or conflict resolution. Dividing the team of 60 full-time teachers by the four time periods allows 15 teachers, or one-fourth of the staff, to be scheduled for a 10-day session of planning and/or staff development every two years.

During this 10-day session, students normally assigned to these teachers can be regrouped according to needs and interests. Activities involving a large group of students, such as the production of a musical, can be scheduled during this period. The two-week session also can serve as time for students to complete mini-courses, participate in community service projects, take part in internship programs, or devote concentrated time to preparing for final class exhibitions (Sizer, 1992). Field trips can be taken during this period without having students miss classroom instructional time. Students lagging behind in their studies can use this time to catch up.

How can we cover 100% of the students for 10 days with 75% of the faculty?

There is one major question regarding this plan: How can we cover 100% of the students for 10 days with 75% of the faculty? This is not as difficult to accomplish as it might seem. Remember, during any one period in a school in which faculty teach five of seven periods, 28.6% (two of seven) teachers are not working with students. To free 25% of the faculty for staff development, class size must be increased and/or the amount of planning time reduced for the remaining 75% of the teachers who instruct during the 10-day term.

For example, in the previously mentioned school of 1,000 students, the average section size would be approximately 23 students. [Calculations for teachers teaching five of seven periods—7 class periods offered x 1,000 students = 7,000 periods; 60 teachers x 5 instructional periods = 300 teaching periods;

7,000/300 = 23 students (average class size).] If the remaining 75% of the teachers took no planning time for the short term, average section size would actually be reduced to 22! [Calculations for 75% of teachers teaching all periods—45 teachers x 7 periods = 315 periods; 7,000/315 = 22 students (average class size).]

If teachers retained one daily planning period, class size would increase to 26; and if two preparation periods per teacher were maintained, class size would increase to 31. [Calculations for 75% of teachers having one planning period—45 teachers x 6 periods = 270 teaching periods; 7,000/270 = 26 students.] [Calculations for 75% of teachers having two periods = 225 teaching periods; 7,000/225 = 31 students.] Thus, by teaching for three 10-day short terms with a slight increase in class size and/or a slight decrease in planning time, teachers gain 10 days of time for staff development and curriculum development every two years, without sending the students home.

VARIATIONS OF THE 80(10)-80(10) PLAN

The 80(10)-80(10) plan outlined above can be adapted to suit a school's goals and priorities. For instance, a 75(15)-75(15) plan would function the same as the previous plan, except that the core instructional periods (terms 1 and 3) would be reduced to 75 days and the block of time (terms 2 and 4) for teacher planning and other student activities extended to 15 (Canady & Rettig, 1993). This plan would provide teachers with three weeks of non-classroom time, which could be devoted to staff development or curriculum design.

Another variation of the same theme would be a 40(5)-40(5)-40(5)-40(5) plan, which would provide students a week every quarter to catch up or participate in enrichment activities. With this plan, all teachers could be released from classroom duties five days every year. Providing annual five-day released periods for all teachers also can be accomplished in the 80(10)-80(10) plan if each 10-day session is broken into two five-day blocks, thus creating an 80(5)(5)-80(5)(5) plan.

THE 20-DAY INSTRUCTIONAL TERM

Another plan breaks each 90-day semester into 20-day instructional terms with two- or three-day planning/study periods between terms: 20(2)-20(3)-20(2)-20(3). This pattern then would be repeated for the second half of the school year. This schedule can be viewed as a semester plan with 80 core instructional days, or as a quarter plan with 40 core instructional days. Each two- or three-day time period scheduled at the end of a 20-day session can be utilized in the same fashion as the planning periods mentioned previously.

Dividing the school year into eight "chunks" of 20(2) or 20(3) time periods provides opportunities for one-fourth of the teachers to be scheduled for released time twice a year for two or three days. With careful planning, schedules can be devised to provide common planning time for teachers on the same team, in the same department, or with the same interest.

Provisions could be made to provide common released time for all teachers by common subject areas.

If this plan were to be followed throughout a school district, provisions could be made to provide common released time for all teachers by common subject areas, thus having predetermined days that might be used for districtwide staff development or curriculum planning. Schools that incorporate peer coaching into their staff development models can schedule released time for coaching partners to observe each other. One teacher can observe his or her partner during the first two-day planning period with the roles of observer/observee reversed during the next three-day period.

While selected teachers are scheduled to be off for either two- or three-day periods, students can be organized into groups according to identified needs or interests. Students who have not completed all of their course requirements, or who are experiencing difficulty in their classes, can be assigned to groups receiving special instructional assistance.

For example, some students might need extra time or assistance to conduct labs, complete research papers, or make up work missed during an absence. Students who do not have computers in their homes can use this time to work in the computer lab. Those who spend many of their after-school hours employed or caring for children might need this extra time just to keep up.

Figure 2
Expanded Teacher Planning in a Rotating Seven-Day Cycle

Days / Daily Class Periods	Day 1 Mon.	Day 2 Tues.	Day 3 Wed.	Day 4 Thurs.	Day 5 Fri.	Day 6 Mon.	Day 7 Tues.
1	1	2	3	4	5	6	7
2	1	2	3	4	5	6	7
3	1	2	3	4	5	6	7
4	2	3	4	5	6	7	1
5	3	4	5	6	7	1	2
6	4	5	6	7	2	1	3
7	6	5	7	1	2	3	4

Example: The shaded areas show how a teacher with planning time scheduled for class periods one and five would have planning time arranged over a seven-day cycle.

SCHEDULING EXTENDED TIME FOR STAFF DEVELOPMENT DURING THE SCHOOL DAY

The schedules discussed previously have used the entire school day as the unit of time for planning. The number of possible scheduling plans is extended further when the unit of time is reduced to hours or periods in a day. Single class periods can be combined to provide larger blocks of instructional time for students and extended periods of planning and staff development time for teachers.

Expanded class periods provide teachers with opportunities to involve students in projects, labs, debates, or even minifield trips—activities that usually are prohibited by lack of time; they also give teachers the opportunity to include a variety of instructional strategies in their teaching. With extended planning periods, teachers can explore new technologies, read professional literature, or observe colleagues.

Figure 2 illustrates a block schedule that has been designed for these purposes. Again, we refer to a school in which teachers instruct five or seven periods. When the teacher planning time is extended, as indicated in Figure 2, each teacher receives two triple-period blocks of planning time within each seven-day cycle.

For instance, in the seven-day cycle, a teacher assigned first and fifth planning periods would have a three-period planning block on days one and five. On days two and six, this same teacher would have another extended block of two periods for planning. A single planning period would be provided on days three and seven, with two nonadjacent periods on day four.

In schools using the semester plan in which there are four blocks, each having four weeks of instruction (the 4/4 semester plan), students complete four courses each semester and have one block for planning. Thus, it is possible to give teachers extended planning time on a rotating cycle (See Chapter 7, Canady & Rettig, 1995). For example, a full day of staff development can be arranged for each teacher every four weeks if the schedule shown in Figure 3 were followed.

All teachers assigned planning during the Course 4 block would have a 90-minute planning session during Block 4 on Monday, Tuesday, Thursday, and Friday. On Wednesday during Week 1, all teachers assigned to teach during Block 1 would work all day with their students in Course 1 classes; on Wednesday of Week 2, teachers assigned to teach during Block 2 would work all day with their students in Course 2 classes; on Wednesday of Week 3 teachers assigned to teach during Block 3 would work all day with students in Course 3 classes; and on Wednesday of the fourth week, all teachers with planning scheduled for Block 4 would have a full day for personal planning or staff development. It is important to remember that one-fourth of staff members would be released each Wednesday in the cycle, depending on which block is their assigned planning time.

Figure 3
Extended Teacher Planning Blocks in the 4/4 Semester Plan
One Day for Teacher Planning Every Four Weeks

	Monday	Tuesday	Wednesday				Thursday	Friday
			W1	W2	W3	W4		
Block 1	Course 1	Course 1	C1	C2	C3	C4	Course 1	Course 1
Block 2	Course 2	Course 2	C1	C2	C3	C4	Course 2	Course 2
Lunch			Lunch					
Block 3	Course 3	Course 3	C1	C2	C3	C4	Course 3	Course 3
Block 4	Course 4	Course 4	C1	C2	C3	C4	Course 4	Course 4

W = Week
C = Course
Example: The shaded portion illustrates planning blocks for 25 percent of the teachers; the remaining 75 percent of the teachers would be distributed equally among the three remaining instructional blocks.

When considering these schedules, recognize that the expanded planning time for teachers translates into extended instructional periods for students. With this flexible schedule, teachers have time to include a variety of instructional strategies, activities, projects, and experiences designed to promote student involvement.

The primary benefit for both teachers and students is the provision of extended blocks of time for planning, teaching, and learning. Rather than using these schedules for the entire school year, it may be better to schedule classes in this manner during designated times throughout the school year, such as once each grading period, when extended planning or instructional time is most needed.

CONCLUSION

As those in charge of scheduling begin to visualize time as a resource that can be manipulated, they can develop schedules similar to those described above, based upon the goals and objectives of their schools. Principals and teacher leaders who place a high priority on staff development can build time within the teaching day and/or year for teachers to participate in professional growth opportunities without sacrificing instructional time for students. In doing so, they will send a clear signal to teachers that the learning process is valued for both teachers and students.

REFERENCES

Adler, M., & Van Doren, C. (1984). The conduct of seminars. In M. Alder (Ed.), *The Paideia program: An educational syllabus* (pp. 15–31). New York: Macmillan.

Canady, R. L., & Retting, M. D. (1995). *Block scheduling: A catalyst for change in high schools*. Princeton, NJ: Eye on Education.

Canady, R. L. (1994). High school alternative scheduling to enhance teaching and learning. *The Video Journal of Education* [video], 4(2).

Canady, R. L., & Rettig, M. D. (1993). Unlocking the lockstep high school schedule. *Phi Delta Kappan, 75*(4), 310–314.

Guskey, T. R. (1986). Staff development and the process of teacher change. *Educational Researcher, 15*(5), 5–12.

Joyce, B., & Showers, B. (1988). *Student achievement through staff development.* New York: Longman. [Second edition, 1995]

Lieberman, A., & Miller, L. (1992). Professional development of teachers. In M. Alkin (Ed.), *Encyclopedia of Educational Research* (pp. 1045–1053). New York: Macmillan.

Little, J. W. (1985). *School success and staff development in urban desegregated schools: A summary of recently completed research.* Paper presented at the annual meeting of the American Educational Research Association, Los Angeles, CA.

Loucks-Horsley, S., Harding, C. K., Arbukle, M. A., Murray, L. B., Dubea, C., & Williams, M. K. (1987). *Continuing to learn: A guidebook for teacher development.* Andover, MA: Regional Laboratory for Educational Improvement of the Northeast & Islands.

National Commissison on Time and Learning. (1994). *Prisoners of time: Report of the National Education Commission on Time and Learning.* Washington, DC: U.S. Government Printing Office.

Sizer, T. (1992). *Horace's school.* Boston: Houghton Mifflin.

What Else?

No one has ever had an idea in a dress suit.—Sir Frederick G. Banting

ew educational innovations appear on the scene unchallenged. In the case of block scheduling, which appears to be a radical shuffling of the traditional schedule, it is only natural that all sides of the issue be explored. If schools are to make long-term commitments to change of this magnitude, those making the decision must, in good conscience, know the expected results of the effort. The stakeholders must believe that the innovation helps engineer their long-term goals, aims, and objectives. To close this collection of articles on block scheduling, the final piece actually circles back to the opening challenge—to block or not to block.

In this final discussion, Clifford A. Baylis, Jr., frames a study around the overriding issue of student performance. Does block scheduling impact positively on student learning? Specifically, the study looks at student attitudes, anxieties, and specific learning behaviors. Although the results of the study, in its limited version, favor block scheduling in the above-mentioned areas, the discussion reveals other related issues of possible interest to the reader.

Finally, Joseph M. Carroll, the father of the Copernican Plan, revisits his plan in order to evaluate its effectiveness. Documenting data from eight very different high schools, Carroll leaves no doubt that the advantages of macroscheduling are overwhelming (for example, reduced drop-out rates, increases in academic achievement, and improved problem-solving skills). In fact, he emphatically calls for reform—for a Copernican Revolution— when he states, "There is no professional reason for delay; . . . continuing with traditional . . . structures(s) raises the serious question of professional malpractice."

In sum, this collection is but a beginning in the search for answers to our questions about block scheduling. What?, So What?, Now What?, and What Else? simply create the framework for further reading on the concept and on-going discussions about block scheduling and all of its ramifications. However, it is hoped that this collection will provide a foundation for fruitful discussions and future investigations into the innovative organizational approach known as block scheduling.

Summary of an Investigation into the Relative Effects on Student Performance on a "Block" vs. "Non-Block" Scheduled Developmental Semester

Clifford A. Baylis, Jr.

D ESCRIPTION
Beginning with the Fall 1980 Semester, a Block Scheduled Developmental Semester was offered for the first time at the Boyce Campus of the Community College of Allegheny County. The Block Scheduled Developmental Semester was composed of a block of three integrated courses (9 credits): Man, Time and Social Change (Social Science Elective); Basic Writing Techniques (Developmental English Course); and College Reading and Study Skills (Social Science Elective). All students in the "Block" were registered for specifically designated sections of each of the three courses. In addition, most students also registered for at least one other course in their chosen program of studies.

DESIGN
An Experimental/Control group pretest-posttest design was used for the purpose of data collection relative to analysis of comparative effects on student performance.

A paper presented to the Developmental Education Committee at the Allegheny County College, Monroeville, Penn., February 15, 1983, ED244711.
© 1983 by Clifford A. Baylis, Jr. Reprinted with permission.

OUTCOMES

Block scheduled students' (Experimental group) pretest measures of attitudes (Table 1), anxieties (Table 2) and 17 specific learning behaviors (Table 3) showed no statistically significant differences when compared to the Control group, i.e., the Control and Experimental groups were equivalent at the start of the semester, thus any differences observed at the end of the semester had a high probability of being accounted for in terms of the difference in the treatment. Differences between the Control and Experimental groups on the posttests showed statistically significant advantages for the Experimental group on almost all variables observed. The Semantic Differential, the instrument used to measure attitude change, showed a statistically significant difference favoring the Experimental group at the .005 level of confidence on three of the five scales used (Table 4). Posttest scores on the Leaning Behavior Inventory, the instrument used to measure learning behavior changes relative to 17 factors, showed a statistically significant difference favoring the Experimental group at the .05 level of confidence on 9 of the 17 scales used (Table 5). Finally, posttest scores on the Anxiety Survey, the instrument used to measure learner anxiety, showed differences favoring the Experimental group; however, there were statistically significant differences in only two of the seven scales used (Table 6).

Other indices used also tended to favor the experimental group, e.g., the dropout rate for block scheduled students was 20% and for non-block scheduled students it was 32.5% (Table 7); the absentee rate for block students was 4.2% as compared to the non-block students absentee rate of 13.5% (Table 8); the Q.P.A. earned by block students was higher (statistically significant at the .005 level) than the Q.P.A. earned by the non-block students (Table 9); finally, there were no statistically significant differences between the groups when the "Iowa Basic Reading Test" was used as the posttest measure of improvement in reading skills (Table 10).

In summary, the use of the Block Scheduled Developmental Semester as a strategy for increasing student success seems to be supported by the data.

Table 1
Semantic Differential

Pre-Mean Scores and Variance of Block Students and
Pre-Mean Scores and Variance of Non-Block Students

n = 22/36

	Pre-Test Block			Pre-Test Non-Block			
	$\overline{X}$	s	s^2	$\overline{X}$	s	s^2	t
Studying	24.68	5.55	30.85	25.33	5.30	28.06	.40
Teachers	29.18	5.10	25.97	29.58	6.76	45.69	.26
Myself	29.86	4.75	22.57	29.00	5.97	35.61	.61
Tests	23.41	6.64	44.10	22.86	7.03	49.40	.30
Classes	29.45	6.32	39.88	28.22	5.37	28.84	.76
Totals	27.32	2.71	7.34	26.00	2.53	6.41	.94

* *p*   .05/d.f. = 21/35
** *p*   .01/d.f. = 21/35
*** *p*   .005/d.f. = 21/35

Table 2
Anxiety Survey

Pre-Mean Scores and Variance of Block Students and
Pre-Mean Scores and Variance of Non-Block Students

n = 22/36

	Pre-Test Block			Pre-Test Non-Block			
	$\overline{X}$	s	s^2	$\overline{X}$	s	s^2	t
Calls Upon	3.00	.80	.64	2.89	.69	.49	.52
Studying Chapter	2.73	.62	.38	2.69	.74	.55	.20
Announce Test	3.41	1.03	1.06	2.83	.99	.97	2.07*
Study for Test	3.09	1.12	1.26	2.97	1.01	1.03	.40
Take Test	3.36	1.11	1.23	3.06	.94	.89	1.03
Test Mistakes	3.14	.97	.94	3.03	.87	.75	.44
Surprise Test	3.91	.90	.81	3.33	.62	.39	2.52**
Totals	3.23	.35	.12	2.97	.19	.43	1.86*

* p   .05/d.f. = 21/35
** p   .01/d.f. = 21/35
*** p   .005/d.f. = 21/35

Table 3
Learning Behavior Inventory

Pre-Mean Scores and Variance of Block Students and
Pre-Mean Scores and Variance of Non-Block Students

n=22/36

	Pre-Test Block			Pre-Test Non-Block			
	$\overline{X}$	s	s^2	$\overline{X}$	s	s^2	t
Attends Class	4.73	.69	.47	4.98	.16	.03	1.79*
Pays Attention	4.23	.60	.36	4.44	.60	.36	1.24
Takes Class Notes	4.18	.72	.51	4.14	.95	.89	.20
Organizes Class Notes	3.55	.99	.98	4.03	1.04	1.08	1.85*
Underlines Text	2.81	1.37	1.79	2.75	1.19	1.41	.17
Takes Text Notes	3.09	1.35	1.81	3.36	1.21	1.45	.77
Reorganizes Text Notes	2.77	1.24	1.54	3.47	1.36	1.86	.20
Relates Text Notes	3.23	1.17	1.36	3.61	1.19	1.40	1.23
Ideas in Own Words	3.68	.92	.86	3.97	.99	.97	1.12
Completes Work	4.64	.57	.32	4.36	.75	.56	1.65*
Asks Class Questions	2.95	1.36	1.86	3.19	1.02	1.05	.73
Answers Class Questions	2.91	1.40	1.54	3.14	.89	.79	.77
Asks for Help	3.91	1.12	1.26	3.81	1.08	1.16	.36
Works Co-operatively	4.41	.83	.70	4.14	1.03	1.06	1.13
Tests Self	3.14	1.25	1.57	2.86	1.25	1.56	.85
Studies with Others	2.18	1.30	1.51	2.42	1.36	1.85	.65
Takes Tests	3.95	.77	.59	4.28	.87	.76	1.50
Totals	3.55	.72	.52	3.70	.67	.44	.88

* p .05/d.f.=21/35
** p .01/d.f.=21/35
*** p .005/d.f.=21/35

Table 4
Semantic Differential

Post-Mean Scores and Variance of Block Students and
Post-Mean Scores and Variance of Non-Block Students

n = 22/36

	Post-Test Block			Post-Test Non-Block			
	$\overline{X}$	s	s^2	$\overline{X}$	s	s^2	t
Studying	28.73	5.46	29.83	24.23	5.73	32.79	2.78**
Teachers	32.95	4.88	23.86	32.23	5.44	29.64	.48
Myself	33.73	4.52	20.47	29.54	5.31	28.17	2.95***
Tests	31.27	5.66	32.02	24.88	8.76	76.72	3.04***
Classes	30.59	7.26	52.78	29.50	6.49	42.10	.55
Totals	31.57	1.72	2.98	28.08	3.05	9.29	6.98***

    * p .05/d.f. = 21/25
   ** p .01/d.f. = 21/25
  *** p .005/d.f. = 21/25

Table 5
Learning Behavior Inventory

Post-Mean Scores and Variance of Block Students and
Post-Mean Scores and Variance of Non-Block Students

n=22/36

	Post-Test Block			Post-Test Non-Block			
	$\overline{X}$	s	s^2	$\overline{X}$	s	s^2	t
Attends Class	4.73	.45	.20	4.50	.64	.40	1.35
Pays Attention	4.86	.34	.12	4.54	.63	.40	1.88*
Takes Class Notes	4.68	.70	.49	4.12	1.15	1.33	2.15*
Organizes Class Notes	4.14	.76	.57	3.65	1.07	1.15	1.88*
Underlines Text	3.45	1.08	1.16	2.58	1.52	2.32	2.35*
Takes Text Notes	3.50	1.12	1.25	2.81	1.30	1.69	2.03*
Reorganizes Text Notes	3.55	1.23	1.52	2.96	1.34	1.81	1.59
Relates Text Notes	3.73	1.09	1.98	3.00	1.39	1.92	1.78*
Ideas in Own Words	4.09	.95	.90	3.46	1.12	1.25	2.10*
Completes Work	4.63	.48	.23	4.31	.91	.83	1.60
Asks Class Questions	3.68	1.33	1.76	3.73	1.35	1.81	.13
Answers Class Questions	3.86	1.03	1.03	3.46	1.08	1.17	1.25
Asks for Help	4.18	1.15	1.33	4.08	1.03	1.07	.31
Works Co-operatively	4.55	.66	.43	4.35	.92	.84	.91
Tests Self	3.32	1.18	1.40	3.35	1.14	1.30	.09
Studies with Others	2.41	1.15	1.33	1.85	1.03	1.05	1.75*
Takes Tests	4.27	.75	.56	4.27	.90	.81	0
Totals	3.99	.62	.38	3.59	.74	.55	2.00*

   * p .05/d.f.=21/35
  ** p .01/d.f.=21/35
*** p .005/d.f.=21/35

Table 6
Anxiety Survey

Post-Mean Scores and Variance of Block Students and
Post-Mean Scores and Variance of Non-Block Students

n= 22/26

	Post-Test Block			Post-Test Non-Block			
	$\overline{X}$	s	s^2	$\overline{X}$	s	s^2	t
Calls Upon	2.09	.73	.54	2.81	.83	.69	3.27***
Studying Chapter	2.14	.76	.57	2.27	.76	.58	.60
Announce Test	2.86	1.06	1.12	2.80	1.00	1.00	.20
Study for Test	2.45	1.08	1.16	2.96	1.09	1.19	1.60
Take Test	2.64	.93	.87	2.96	1.09	1.19	1.07
Test Mistakes	2.55	.58	.34	3.08	1.07	1.15	2.21*
Surprise Test	2.86	1.06	1.12	3.23	.93	.87	1.32
Totals	2.51	.29	.08	2.83	.29	.53	.79

* *p* .05/d.f. = 21/25
** *p* .01/d.f. = 21/25
*** *p* .005/d.f. = 21/25

Table 7

Retention of Fall 1980 Block and Non-Block Students for the Spring 1981 Semester

n=25/40

Registered Fall 1980	Block Retained Spring 1981		Drop-outs		Registered Fall 1980	Non-Block Retained Spring 1981		Drop-outs	
Number	No.	%	No.	%	Number	No.	%	No.	%
25	20	80	5	20	40	27	67.5	13	32.5

Table 8

Block and Non-Block Student Attendance Patterns

n=14/11*

	Block				Non-Block			
Number Students	—0— Absences	Total Absences	Absentee %	Number Students	—0— Absences	Total Absences	Absentee %
14	4	26	4.20	11	0	60	13.45

*One Block and Three Non-Block Students stopped attending class and were not included in data computation.

Table 9

Comparison of Block and Non-Block Student Mean Q.P.A. for Fall 1980 Semester

n=24/37

Block Q.P.A.			Non-Block Q.P.A.			
$\overline{X}$	s	s^2	$\overline{X}$	s	s^2	t
2.31	.95	.89	1.95	1.14	1.13	4.5***

*** p   .005/d.f. = 23/36

Table 10

Comparison of Block and Non-Block Student Raw Score on the Iowa Basic Reading Test: Test 2, Comprehension

n=21/28

	Pre-Test			Post-Test			
	$\overline{X}$	s	s^2	$\overline{X}$	s	s^2	t
Block	30.45	2.63	6.92	32.50	5.52	30.47	1.01*
Non-Block	28.40	7.79	60.71				.53**

* Block Student Pre-Post Mean Scores
** Block Student Pre-Mean Score and Non-Block Student
    Pre-Mean Score

The Copernican Plan Evaluated: The Evolution of a Revolution

by Joseph M. Carroll

I have bad new and good news. The bad news is that our schools, particularly our high schools, are in serious trouble and may be replaced by new institutions of choice, both public and private. Our education efforts are failing to produce either a work force capable of competing with those of other industrialized nations or a citizenry capable of meeting its critically important responsibilities under our form of government. The good news is that all we have to do is apply what research tells us about better instruction and we can meet those economic and civic demands. How? Let me start from the beginning.

EVOLUTION OF A COPERNICAN CHANGE
When I was the assistant superintendent for research, budget, and legislation for the District of Columbia Public Schools in the mid-1960s, we found ourselves with a financial windfall. A proposal was made and approved that the money be put toward a remedial summer school for academically troubled students. The students in that summer school studied math and English for four hours a day, five days a week, for six weeks—a typical summer program.

What was atypical was that we evaluated quite carefully. Based on traditional pre- and posttests for these students, the average student's gains were equal to the gains achieved in

From *Phi Delta Kappan,* vol. 76, no. 2, October 1994, pp. 105–113.

about two years in regular classes. And the teachers' reports on the climate in the classroom, attendance, and so on were equally good. We were elated. But then we were struck by a very logical question. If we can do this well in 30 four-hour summer classes in nonair-conditioned D.C. public schools, why can't we do better in our traditional 180-day programs during the regular school year? We thought of many possible reasons, but my only conclusion was that we probably knew a lot more about teaching than we did about how students learn.

I followed up on this experience when I became superintendent of the Los Alamos (New Mexico) Public Schools in the early 1970s. There we were able to offer students regular credit-bearing high school courses on a nonremedial basis as part of our summer school program. Each class met in a four-hour "macroclass" each day, five days per week, for six weeks—which was about 20% less total time than was provided for a course under the school's traditional 180-day school year. This fact was never questioned, but it interested me greatly. The teachers in the summer program had been asked to apply the same standards that they used to grade their students during the regular year and to let us know if the summer students could not meet the district's usual standards in this format. Again the results were excellent, and the teachers reported exceptionally good relations with the summer students; the "coke breaks" were enjoyable.

> We probably knew a lot more about teaching than we did about how students learn.

But what to do with this information? We seemed to have a solution looking for a problem!

The "problem" surfaced when I was superintendent of the Masconomet Regional School District in Massachusetts. A tax limitation referendum had passed in 1980, and by 1982 our district had lost about a sixth of its teaching staff. Keeping the program intact was going to be very difficult. Necessity breeds invention, and it occurred to me that "macro scheduling" might address this problem. Thus began a long planning process. In the fall of 1983 I distributed a document to the staff and school community called "The Copernican Plan: A Concept Paper Concerning the Restructuring of Secondary Education at the

Masconomet Regional School District." I had finally put it all together.

However, my enthusiasm was shared by few members of the Masconomet community, which was no surprise. "Restructuring" wasn't a hot topic at that time. Masconomet had an excellent academic reputation, and there weren't too many people who felt the need for major change. Still, in 1989 we were able to initiate a pilot program at Masconomet to test the basic Copernican concepts. But before discussing that pilot program, let me provide an overview of the Copernican Plan.

> We were able to initiate a pilot program at Masconomet to test the basic Copernican concepts.

THE COPERNICAN PLAN

First, why call it the Copernican Plan? Nicolaus Copernicus was a 16th century scholar whose major contribution was his explanation of the movements of the planets. Planetary movements had been studied for centuries. Copernicus' contribution was simple, but fundamental. If planetary movements are studied assuming the sun to be the center of the universe, all measurements make sense. Study them on the assumption that the earth is the center, and nothing makes sense. Nevertheless, Copernicus' theory encountered tremendous resistance and was viewed as dangerous since it challenged articles of faith concerning creation and man's role on earth.

The Copernican Plan also challenges what has become an article of education faith—the Carnegie unit, which has dominated the structure of secondary schools for almost a century. Under the Carnegie structure, teachers typically teach five classes, each approximately 45 minutes in length, and thus deal with about 125 students each day. Too often teachers deal with 150 or even 180 students per day. Virtually all the research concerning better instructional practice emphasizes greater individualization of instruction.[1] But secondary teachers are caught in a structure that fosters lecture-centered, large-group-oriented instruction and sharply limits their efforts to individualize.[2]

The Carnegie structure has an adverse impact on students as well. Students typically enroll in six courses that meet daily during a 180-day school year. In a typical high school, which has seven periods plus a home room and a lunch period, students will be in nine different locations pursuing nine very different activities during the course of an approximately 6 $^1/_2$-hour school day. Regardless of subject, students are taught in classes lasting approximately 45 minutes. This is an impersonal, procrustean structure that prevents the teacher from working closely with each student. Indeed, a student may go through an entire day—or several days—without having a meaningful interaction with a teacher. In summation, the Carnegie structure is a system under which teachers can't teach effectively and students can't learn effectively.

The Copernican Plan fundamentally changes the way schools use time. For example, classes are taught in much longer periods (90 minutes, two hours, or four hours per day), and they meet for only part of the school year (30 days, 45 days, 60 days, or 90 days). Thus students are enrolled in significantly fewer classes each day, and teachers deals with significantly fewer classes and students each day. The schedule change is not an end in itself but a means to create a classroom environment that fosters vastly improved relationships between teachers and students and that provides much more manageable workloads for both teachers and students. In theory, the outcome should be schools that are more successful.

The Copernican Plan projects the following specific advantages:

> Virtually every high school in this nation can decrease its average class size by 20 percent; increase its course offerings or number of sections by 20 percent; reduce the total number of students with whom a teacher works each day by 60 to 80 percent; provide students with regularly scheduled seminars dealing with complex issues; establish a flexible, productive instructional environment that allows effective mastery learning as well as other practices recommended by research; get students to master 25 to 30 percent more information in addition to what they learn in the seminars; and do all of this within the approximately present levels of funding.[3]

The Copernican Plan proposed other changes as well: evaluation based on a mastery credit system, individual learning plans, multiple diplomas and a new credit system with two types of credits, and the dejuvenilizing of our high schools. But the success of these changes depends on the fundamental Copernican change of the classroom environment.

EVALUATION

The Copernican Plan is just that—a plan, albeit one based on research and nontraditional experience. Will it work? How do we test these Copernican concepts?

The productive unit in education is the school, and that is the natural laboratory in which to test the effectiveness of educational proposals. Research concepts and techniques should be used in evaluating instructional programs—but, to be effective, educators must exercise informed judgment about the meaning of research findings. Moreover, it is important to remember that a decision not to change means that what is being done now is better than any alternative. In other words, when we consider changes, we should be sure that the present program meets the same standards as we are applying to proposed changes. And we should always keep in mind that, *while it is possible to change without improving, it is impossible to improve without changing.*

> The productive unit in education is the school, and that is the natural laboratory in which to test the effectiveness of educational proposals.

The following sections will present evaluations of the impact of implementing the Copernican Plan in eight very different high schools that use seven different Copernican schedules. There is one question that is fundamental to all eight evaluations: Do students function as well and learn as effectively under a Copernican structure as they do under a traditional Carnegie structure? This question goes to the heart of educational accountability, *for nothing—absolutely nothing—has happened in education until it happens to a student.*

In these evaluations, the baseline data—the information against which progress or lack of progress must be measured—

consist of data about student performance under traditional, Carnegie schedules; the experimental variable is the implementation of a Copernican schedule. The impact of that experimental variable is measured by comparing the baseline performance data with performance data from students functioning and learning under a Copernican schedule, and research methodologies are used in analyzing the data and interpreting the results.

> It was clear from the beginning that an objective outside evaluation of the program would be necessary.

THE FIRST COPERNICAN PILOT PROGRAM

In 1989 Masconomet Regional High School in Boxford, Massachusetts, began to implement the first Copernican pilot program, which was named the Renaissance Program. It was a program of "choice"; that is, students volunteered to be in it. The plan was for the program to begin with the ninth grade and to add a grade each year, contingent on favorable evaluations. The students who selected the pilot program became known as "Renpro" students; similarly, students who decided to stay with the traditional program became known as "Tradpro" students.

The Renpro schedule divided the year into three trimesters of 60 days each. Students following this schedule took two 100-minute classes each morning for a full trimester, for a total of 100 hours per class. In the second year of the program, each morning class met for a total of 118 hours. Since the traditional classes met for 46 minutes a day for 181 days per year, or 139 hours, a Renpro class met for about 25% less time, but students still earned full course credit. Renpro students completed six morning classes (two each trimester) per year, and in the afternoon they could take traditionally scheduled electives and participate in a seminar program. Renpro teachers taught two classes a day.

These changes were most controversial. Thus it was clear from the beginning that an objective outside evaluation of the program would be necessary. An evaluation committee representing both supporters and critics of the pilot program was formed. The committee identified the questions that needed to be answered, interviewed potential evaluators, and then selected an outstanding team of evaluators from Harvard University. The validity of the Renaissance Program and, to a very considerable extent, of the Copernican Plan would be either established or destroyed by this team's findings concerning what happened to students as a result of this Copernican change. The evaluators were aboard and working before the program began.

In order to answer the questions that had been generated by the school's evaluation committee, the Harvard team used a number of different evaluative approaches. They gave questionnaires to Renpro and Tradpro parents, students, and teachers so that they could compare responses from the groups. They had a strong basis for making academic comparisons, because the Masconomet program had been deliberately set up so that the curriculum, the midterm exams, and the finals for all courses were exactly the same for both groups.

THE FINDINGS
Here are the questions that were presented to the evaluators, the predictions of the programs' critics, and the evaluators' findings.

1. Will the students be able to function effectively in long "macroclasses" of about two hours?

Prediction
Many critics predicted that all but perhaps the most able students would get "burned out" trying to concentrate on one subject for so long a time.

The Findings
The evaluators reviewed the two years of student data and came to the following conclusions:

> Renaissance students were better known by their teachers, were responded to with more care, did more writing, pursued issues in greater depth, enjoyed their classes more, felt more challenged, and gained deeper understandings. Students can move from classes of 46 minutes to those of 188 minutes and back again. They are more flexible when it comes to length of class than is normally assumed, although Renaissance students preferred the

longer class periods. Concentration on only two classes in much longer periods, aided by reduced class size, markedly improves the interpersonal relationships that develop between teacher and student, and between student and student.[4]

2. Will the teachers find the intensity of teaching classes for roughly two hours draining?

Prediction
Again, there were those who predicted that teachers would suffer burnout from the new schedule.

The Findings
A high level of unanimity among the Renpro teachers is reflected in this summary statement, which is based on questionnaires and interviews:

> Renaissance teachers were excited about their teaching. They felt rejuvenated and believed they were teaching students more productively than ever. We learned that teachers of any level of seniority who get involved in developing a new program can become rededicated to teaching and give more time and energy to their students than previously. Simple changes in the length of class periods and in class size can in themselves invite teachers to rethink their pedagogical styles.

It should be noted that the Tradpro teachers felt stressed by the competition presented by the Renpro pilot. Both sets of teachers felt that the competitive pressure created by a partial high school or school-within-a-school approach was a negative factor.

3. Will the students learn as much as they would under the traditional structure?

Prediction
A major objection to the Renpro experiment was that, with approximately 25% fewer total hours per course, the Renpro classes would not be able to "cover" the curriculum.

The Findings

The evaluators started their comparison of the two programs by looking at the mathematics and reading scores of both the Renpro and the Tradpro students as they went into the ninth grade. The Tradpro students entered the ninth grade with significantly higher reading scores and somewhat higher mathematics scores than did the Renpro students.

Here are the evaluators' comments:

> The academic performance of each program was analyzed by comparing the midterm exams of each Renaissance trimester with the midyear exams of the Traditional students, and the final exams of each trimester with the traditional end-of-year exams. Teachers in both programs used the same curriculum, and the same midterm and final exams were administered to students.
>
> Renpro students had significantly fewer hours of class (100 vs. 139 hours in the first year, 118 vs. 139 hours in the second year, and 118 vs. 162 hours for science with the traditional double laboratory period). While there were differences in scores between students in the two programs, these differences essentially balanced out. The results were comparable, even though there were significant differences in "time on task." In addition, Renpro students had more opportunities for academic enrichment (more courses, seminars, independent studies, and foreign language enrichment programs) than did the Tradpro and actually completed 13% more course credits than did Tradpro students.

Specific figures for the test results referred to in the evaluators' comments were as follows: out of 74 comparisons of the two groups' midterm and final examination scores, 49 showed no significant difference between the two groups' performance, 11 showed a significant difference favoring the Renpro students, and 14 showed a significant difference favoring the Tradpro students. Thus it is clear that, although the Renpro students entered the ninth grade looking less able than the Tradpro students, once they were in high school they not only performed as well as the Tradpro students on their examinations but also completed 13% more courses—in addition to a seminar program not taken by the Tradpro students.

4.   Will the students retain as much of what they learn?

Prediction

Critics pointed out that Renpro students could take a course in the first trimester in one year and might not take the next sequential course until the third trimester of the following year— a gap of 15 months as compared to the traditional summer vacation gap of three months. They believed students would forget a great deal more in such a long period and that this would seriously hamper their academic progress.

The Findings

There were really two measures of retention in this evaluation. The first measure was inherent in the structure of this pilot program because Renpro students were required to begin one-third of their courses after a gap of three months since their previous course in the subject (June to September), one-third after a gap of six months (June to December), and one-third after a gap of nine months (June to March). Thus the findings presented in response to question 3 above—that the Renpro students performed as well academically as the Tradpro students—are evidence that the longer gaps between sequential courses were not instructionally significant.

The Harvard evaluators, however, decided to test retention levels for the two programs directly. Here are their findings:

> During the second year, in September, December, and March, comparisons were made of the retention of material studied during the first year. These comparisons, referred to as "gap tests," were administered from three months to 15 months after the courses ended. Even when one takes into account that gap test results were compared without regard to the time lapse between final exam and gap test (which should favor the traditional program), there were no consistent significant differences that favored students in one program over students in the other. The . . . Renaissance and the Traditional program students had comparable levels of retention.

5.   Will there be as much in-depth instruction in the Renaissance Program as in the traditional program?

Prediction
The critics believed that the pressure to "cover" the curriculum in significantly less time would result in superficial learning and that students would not have the chance to address the more complex questions that would help to develop their higher-order thinking and problem-solving skills.

The Findings
A special, well-structured evaluation was designed to test the impact of the Renpro pilot on the higher-order thinking and problem-solving ability of students. The evaluators concluded:

> Oral exams assessing students' capacities for thinking through problems and working cooperatively showed that . . . Renaissance students performed significantly better than Traditional students on these dimensions. When the sign test was applied to these data collectively, the Renpro students performed significantly better than Tradpro students ($p<0.001$).

For those not familiar with statistical concepts, this finding means that if there really were no difference between these two programs in terms of their impact on the development of these skills, the chance of getting a sample of students who scored this differently would be less than one in a thousand. In a profession where one chance in 20 is considered statistically significant, this finding strongly supports the premise that a Copernican-type program will develop higher-order thinking and problem-solving skills in students more effectively than will traditionally structured programs.

The Bottom Line
On all five of these major questions, the Copernican pilot program was found to be significantly more effective than its Tradpro counterpart. The evaluators expressed it this way:

> These results represent a small sample and only two years' experience, and thus cannot be viewed as conclusive. However, it is clear that the assumption that the traditional daily and yearly schedules are the more effective has been seriously challenged. Responsibility for justification now falls on those who favor the

Traditional schedule. Implementing a Copernican-style schedule can be accomplished with the expectation of favorable pedagogical outcomes.

TESTING THE HARVARD TEAM'S CONCLUSIONS

Was the Harvard team right? The evaluations of seven other high schools implementing Copernican schedules should provide the answer. These seven high schools serve students from urban, suburban, and rural communities; they represent many areas of the U.S. and (in one case) Canada. Their enrollments range from about 250 to more than 1,500 students. Most high schools in the U.S. and Canada are similar to one of these seven high schools. What were their experiences with their respective schedules?

Organizing the Evaluations

All seven high schools were able to provide reliable evaluative data on five measures of student performance for each of two years: the last year under a traditional schedule and the first year under a Copernican schedule. All seven schools had changed schedules without significantly changing their curricula or grading standards from those used during the last year of the traditional schedule.

Six of the seven schools moved to a schoolwide Copernican schedule. Other than the normal year-to-year turnover, there were no changes in staffing. Thus year-to-year changes in student performance in these schools cannot be accounted for by the selection of teachers. The seventh school ran a pilot school-within-a-school program, for which teachers volunteered, a factor that might have had a favorable impact on the results.

Since six of these high schools shifted the schedule of the whole school, the participating students were not selected— these were not "choice" schools. The schedule changed, but the socioeconomic backgrounds of the students did not. In the school-within-a-school program, 58% of the participating students had been pre-identified as "at risk." Each high school operated independently of any of the others. If there is consistency in the results obtained in these seven high schools, it is not attributable to common planning or even to communications between them.

The Copernican Factor

The seven high schools present six different versions of a Copernican schedule. Thus the level of implementation of the Copernican concepts varies considerably. How can we determine whether different Copernican schedules have different impacts on student performance?

First, we have to quantify the degree of concentration in the new Copernican schedules. The "Copernican factor" measures this aspect of a program. The Copernican factor is the sum of the number of classes that a typical teacher teaches and the number of classes in which a typical student is enrolled each day. For example, a traditional high school program typically has students taking six classes and teachers teaching five classes per day; the Copernican factor in this case is 11. The seven high schools implemented schedules with Copernican factors ranging from 4 to 14, with a median of 6.5.[5]

Evaluative Factors

The evaluations were designed to address directly the question of whether these high schools improved in terms of five generally accepted measures of climate/conduct and academic mastery. While schools may differ in their policies and practices concerning these five measures, none of them changed their own policies or practices significantly between their last year under a traditional structure and their first year under a Copernican structure. The performance of each of the seven high schools could be compared on each of the five measures—a total of 35 individual evaluations—and it was also possible to compare them on a composite measure that summarized the results for each high school. Let me be specific.

Impact on Student Conduct

The seven schools were evaluated on three measures of student conduct: attendance, suspension rates, and dropout rates. Because attendance and dropout rates must be reported to the state, this information is generated consistently from year to year. Not all states require reporting of suspensions, and two of the seven schools were not able to provide usable data for both years. The key requirement for the evaluation was that the date be reported consistently for each year by each high school, thus reflecting changes in student conduct.

• The impact of the Copernican Plan on *attendance* was not spectacular, but it was positive, with four schools showing improved attendance, two showing declines, and one showing no change.

The reductions in suspension and dropout rates are educationally spectacular.

• Four of the five high schools that were able to provide suspension data for the two years showed reductions in the *rate of suspension*, ranging from 25% to 75% during the first years under a Copernican structure; one high school reported an 11% increase in suspensions. The two schools that could not provide data reported that conduct improved under their respective Copernican schedules, but the baseline data were not available.

• The most significant improvement occurred in the area of *dropout rates*. Six of the seven high schools reported reductions in dropout rates, ranging from 17% to 63%. Three of these six high schools had had serious retention problems, losing from 27% to more than 50% of their students before graduation. The dropout rates of these three schools were reduced by 63%, 58%, and 36%. (One high school's dropout rate increased from 1.6% to 2.6%, which was a 62% increase; small changes can produce large percentages.) The median change for the seven high schools was a 36% reduction in the first year under a Copernican schedule. By way of comparison, a state dropout reduction program in Massachusetts reported an 11% reduction after three years.[6]

Moreover, schools with large numbers of transient students will benefit from the ability to start students in classes two, three, or four times a year. With this kind of schedule, students do not begin classes far behind the other students, and they know that they can complete a full course if they can stay in school for 45, 60, or 90 days; these are significant improvements for these at-risk students.

The reductions in suspension and dropout rates are educationally spectacular. They occur because the Copernican change improves the relationships between teachers and students and provides more manageable workloads for both. It appears that students who know their teachers and feel a part of their classes tend to be less disruptive and to stay in school. No "rocket science" here, just research findings being confirmed in practice.

Impact on Academic Performance

Each school provided data on all final grades in all subjects for the two years being compared. These data were then analyzed in terms of two measures of academic mastery, which were based on two premises. The first premise is that, when a teacher awards a student a high grade, it is evidence that the teacher believes that the student mastered more of the objectives of the course than did a student who received a lower grade. The second premise is that, if students complete more courses successfully, they have mastered more of the school's academic program than would be the case if they had completed fewer courses. (And if these premises aren't true, American education is really in deep trouble!)

> These schools experienced improvements of a magnitude seldom if ever reported from a group of our nation's high schools.

Based on these two premises, estimates of academic mastery were developed for each of the seven high schools. The schools' increases in academic mastery ranged from 0% to 46%. The median increase was 18%. In the cases of two high schools, the year-to-year results with regard to academic mastery were solidly confirmed by the year-to-year scores on strong state/provincial testing programs. Appropriate testing results were not available for the other schools.

COPERNICAN MESSAGES

The major message derived from the evaluations of these seven high schools is that the Harvard evaluation team's conclusion about the Renpro pilot—that schools can implement a Copernican-type schedule with the expectation of "favorable pedagogical outcomes"—was a sound one. Indeed, these schools experienced improvements of a magnitude seldom if ever reported from a group of our nation's high schools.[7]

There are a considerable number of other significant messages generated by these research-based evaluations. Let me summarize some of them.

Copernican or Carnegie?

This article proposes a revolution that is centered on eliminating the procrustean Carnegie unit, which has dominated—and impaired—secondary education for almost a century. The evaluations summarized above analyzed seven schools' data on five measures of student performance. For each school and on each measure, performance during a year under a traditional Carnegie schedule was compared to performance during a year under a Copernican schedule. Since two schools could not provide data for one of the measures, the evaluations included a total of 33 comparisons. Out of those 33, one comparison showed no difference, 27 favored the Copernican schedule and only five favored the traditional schedule. If the choice of schedule really made no difference in student performance, the odds of getting a distribution in the results favoring one of these programs at this level would be less than one in 10,000. Conservatively stated, the odds are thousands to one that students by chance will perform better academically and conduct themselves better under a Copernican structure than they will under a traditional Carnegie structure.

What Copernican Model is Most Effective?

There are many Copernican schedules. Are some more effective than others? It is possible to evaluate the relative effectiveness of different Copernican schedules. First, the schools are ranked, one to seven, on the basis of their respective Copernican factors. Then each school is ranked, one through seven, according to its composite score on the five performance measures. The Copernican factors of these seven schools were found to correlate with their respective composite scores at the 5% level of confidence. This means that, if there really were no relationship between these seven schools' Copernican factors and their composite scores, the odds of getting this distribution of results would be less than one in 20 samples. These data strongly support those models with a lower Copernican factor—that is, schedules that provide longer macroclasses and also provide for teachers and students to deal with significantly fewer classes at a time.

The Importance of Systemic Change

One of the surprising findings of the evaluations was the relatively limited role that staff development played in bringing about Copernican improvements in student performance. Indeed, the high schools that had the poorest change process—one that provided its teachers no opportunity to learn how to adapt instruction to a macroclass—achieved excellent improvements. Conversely, a school with one of the best staff development programs and a good process had the poorest results and was the only school to show no academic improvement. It is interesting to note that the first school had a Copernican factor of 5; the second school had a Copernican factor of 14—the highest among the seven schools. Is this logical? From the viewpoint of some of W. Edwards Deming's research concerning systemic change, it is very logical. Deming found that 85% of an organization's problems are usually caused by the system; only about 15% are related to poor performance of staff. A Copernican change has an impact on every student, teacher, and class on every day—it changes the system. Staff development imposed on an outmoded system will do little to improve classroom practice.

> A Copernican change has an impact on every student, teacher, and class on every day—it changes the system.

Do These Results Square with the Research?

Why should the Copernican Plan work? Many critics sincerely believe that we can't "cover the curriculum" under a Copernican schedule and also believe that the students will forget too much if they are out of class for more than a three-month summer vacation. According to the Harvard team's evaluation, these fears are unfounded. Were the team's findings consistent with other research? An analysis of the research on time, learning, and memory shows that the results obtained by the Harvard evaluation team were predictable.[8] And the research supports the results obtained by the evaluations of the other seven high schools as well.

The Importance of Teachers

One message came through loud and clear. Every favorable outcome reported herein is evidence of the potential effectiveness of teachers, is a tribute to their importance, and provides a special insight into the quality of teaching under a Copernican structure. The concept of the teacher as a "role model"—a notion virtually absent from the current discourse concerning secondary schools and their problems—seems to have reemerged as the teacher dealt with far fewer students for much longer periods of time. Teachers can be immensely effective if they and their students are given a structure that allows them to show what they can do.

> The Copernican Plan stands the traditional practice of curriculum development on its head.

Other Messages

By emphasizing the structure in which the curriculum will be taught rather than the content, scope, or sequence of the curriculum, the Copernican Plan stands the traditional practice of curriculum development on its head. The experience of the individual schools in the evaluations also calls into question the conventional wisdom concerning the change process (e.g., emphasizing sequential steps—strategic planning, analysis of beliefs, defining a vision). Several schools followed more traditional processes (more emphasis on an improved product and less concern about process), and, in one case, if a school had wanted to "do it wrong," it could not have improved on its nonprocess. Yet these schools got very good results.

Finally, the major problem with most efforts to change schools is the failure to plan an evaluation as an integral part of the program and to evaluate in terms of student outcomes. Many good professionals will advise administrators and planning teams not to initiate academic evaluations until the new program is being implemented properly, which could take several years. Our experience does not support that position. New programs should be planned well enough so that there is reason to expect some improvement. The key political and professional question is whether a proposed new program is improving the education of students, based on the measures that the profession and the public will accept as "solid." Those who would change schools must be prepared to answer that question.

OPPORTUNITY FOR A COPERNICAN REVOLUTION

If every high school in the nation—more than 20,000 schools—shifted from a Carnegie-based structure to a Copernican structure, would it make much difference in our schools' ability to meet major national demands for improved student performance? If we look at the national goals for education set forth in Goals 2000 (the Clinton Administration's version of American 2000) and look at the results reported in the evaluations of the Copernican experiments—a reduction in dropout rates, an increase in academic mastery, and improved problem-solving skills—we can see that a relatively simple Copernican change could take us a long way toward meeting these goals. And this change in structure should be achievable in two to three years. There is no professional reason for delay; in fact, continuing with the present traditional Carnegie structure raises the serious question of professional malpractice. There is no economic reason for delay. The change in structure—the systemic change—will get significantly better results than will be possible under the traditional structure.

For a fundamental change of virtually all our nation's high schools to occur within a few years would be revolutionary, indeed. But a revolution is coming. It will either be a revolutionary change in the responsiveness of those currently in control of our schools or it will be a revolution focused on the creation of alternatives to the present system.

Many of our critics say that the secondary schools—and particularly high schools—cannot change significantly, and the record lends credence to their claim. That claim will not be put to rest by further debate, but only by the actions of thousands of high school teachers, administrators, and board members and the resulting improvement in the performance of their students. The opportunity for a Copernican revolution in secondary education is here. We can do it. And the best part is that we can do it our way. So let's get on with it!

NOTES

1. American Educational Research Association, *Encyclopedia of Educational Research*, 6th ed. (New York: Macmillan, 1992), pp. 613–18.

2. John I. Goodlad, *A Place Called School: Prospects for the Future* (New York: McGraw-Hill, 1984), pp. 105–6.

3. Joseph M. Carroll, *The Copernican Plan: Restructuring the American High School* (Andover, Mass.: Regional Laboratory for Educational Improvement of the Northeast and Islands), p. 15. For a somewhat less detailed explanation of the Copernican Plan, see Joseph M. Carroll, "The Copernican Plan: Restructuring the American High School," *Phi Delta Kappan*, January 1990, p. 358–65.

4. All evaluators' quotations are from Dean K. Whitla, Janine Bempechat, Vito Perrone, and Barbara B. Carroll, "The Masconomet Regional High School Renaissance Program: The First Implementation of the Copernican Plan; the Final Report of the Harvard Evaluation Team," May 1992.

5. In the school with the Copernican factor of 14, students alternated eight classes, four classes one day and four different classes the next day. Teachers alternated six classes, three classes one day and three other classes the next day. Classes alternated for the entire 180-day school year.

6. *Dropout Rates in Massachusetts Public Schools: 1991* (Quincy: Massachusetts Department of Education, March 1993), p. 2.

7. See, for example, Donna E. Muncey and Patrick J. McQuillan, "Preliminary Findings from a Five-Year Study of the Coalition of Essential Schools," *Phi Delta Kappan*, February 1993, pp. 486–89; Michael J. Schmoker and Richard B. Wilson, *Total Quality Education: Profiles of Schools That Demonstrate the Power of Deming's Management Principles* (Bloomington, Ind.: Phi Delta Kappa Educational Foundation, 1993), pp. xiii–xiv, 163–66; and Karen Seashore Louis and Matthew B. Miles, *Improving the Urban High School* (New York: Teachers College Press, 1990), pp. 49–51.

8. See Joseph M. Carroll, *The Copernican Plan Evaluated: The Evolution of a Revolution* (Topsfield, Mass.: Copernican Associates, 1994), pp. 78–84.

Authors

Clifford A. Baylis, Jr., is director of the learning center at the Boyce Campus of the Community College of Allegheny County, cofounder of the Pennsylvania Association of Developmental Education (PADE), curriculum consultant, and researcher on "math anxiety."

Robert Lynn Canady is professor and former chair of the Department of Educational Leadership and Policy Studies at the University of Virginia. His most recent books are *School Policy, Block Scheduling: A Catalyst for Change in High Schools,* and *Teaching in the Block.*

Joseph M. Carroll is senior associate of Copernican Associates in Topsfield, Massachusetts. He is the author of *The Copernican Plan: Restructuring the American High School* and *The Copernican Plan Evaluated: The Evolution of a Revolution.*

Robin Fogarty has taught all levels from kindergarten to college, served as an administrator, and consulted with state departments and ministries of education around the world. She has authored, coauthored, and edited numerous books and articles.

Donald G. Hackmann is an assistant professor of educational leadership in the Department of Leadership and Counseling at Eastern Michigan University, Ypsilanti, Michigan.

Michael D. Rettig is an assistant professor in the School of Education at James Madison University in Virginia. He has worked with over 200 schools on scheduling issues and is coauthor of *Block Scheduling: A Catalyst for Change in High Schools.*

Roger Schoenstein teaches Latin and English at Roy J. Wasson High School in Colorado Springs, Colorado, where he was foreign language chairman for four years. He started teaching public school in 1966, and has taught from sixth grade through college.

Rebecca Shore is an administrator in the Huntington Beach Union High School District and is completing a doctoral dissertation on the California Charter Schools at the University of Southern California.

Brenda Tanner is Assistant Superintendent for Instruction in the Louisa County Schools in Virginia and is studying the staff development needs of teachers in schools with block scheduling as part of her doctoral studies at the University of Virginia.

Acknowledgments

Grateful acknowledgment is made to the following authors and agents for their permission to reprint copyrighted materials.

SECTION 1
The American Association of School Administrators (AASA) for "Organizing Time to Support Learning" by Joseph M. Carroll. From *The School Administrator,* vol. 51, no. 3, pp. 26–28, 30–33, March 1994. Copyright © 1994 by AASA. Reprinted with permission. All rights reserved.

The Association for Supervision and Curriculum Development (ASCD) and Rebecca Shore for "How One High School Improved School Climate" by Rebecca Shore. From *Educational Leadership,* vol. 52, no. 5, pp. 76–78, May 1995. Copyright © 1995 by ASCD. Reprinted with permission. All rights reserved.

The Education Digest for "Making Block Scheduling Work" by Roger Schoenstein. From *The Education Digest,* pp. 15–19, February 1995. Copyright © 1995 by The Education Digest. Reprinted with permission. All rights reserved.

SECTION 2
The Association for Supervision and Curriculum Development (ASCD), Robert Lynn Canady, and Michael D. Rettig for "The Power of Innovative Scheduling" by Robert Lynn Canady and Michael D. Rettig. From *Educational Leadership,* vol. 53, no. 3, pp. 4–10, November 1995. Copyright © 1995 by ASCD. Reprinted with permission. All rights reserved.

The National Association of Elementary School Principals (NAESP) for "Parallel Block Scheduling: A Better Way to Organize a School" by Robert Lynn Canady. From *Principal,* vol. 69, no. 3, pp. 34–36, January 1990. Copyright © 1990 by the NAESP. Reprinted with permission. All rights reserved.

The Education Digest for "The Copernican Plan to Restructure High Schools" by Joseph M. Carroll. From *The Education Digest,* pp. 32–35, September 1990. Copyright © 1990 by The Education Digest. Reprinted with permission. All rights reserved.

The Association for Supervision and Curriculum Development (ASCD) and Donald G. Hackmann for "Ten Guidelines for Implementing Block Scheduling" by Donald G. Hackmann. From *Educational Leadership,* vol. 53, no. 3, pp. 24–27, November 1995. Copyright © 1995 by ASCD. Reprinted with permission. All rights reserved.

SECTION 3

The National Staff Development Council (NSDC) for "Scheduling Time to Maximize Staff Development Opportunities" by Brenda Tanner, Robert L. Canady, and Michael D. Rettig. From *Journal of Staff Development,* vol. 16, no. 4, pp. 14–19, Fall 1995. Copyright © 1995 by NSDC. Reprinted with permission. All rights reserved.

SECTION 4

Clifford A. Baylis, Jr., for "Summary of an Investigation into the Relative Effects on Student Performance on a 'Block' vs. 'Non-Block' Scheduled Developmental Semester" by Clifford A. Baylis, Jr. From a paper presented to the Developmental Education Committee at the Allegheny County Community College, Monroeville, Penn., February 15, 1983. Copyright © 1983 by Clifford A. Baylis, Jr. Reprinted with permission. All rights reserved.

Phi Delta Kappa and Joseph M. Carroll for "The Copernican Plan Evaluated: The Evolution of a Revolution" by Joseph M. Carroll. From *Phi Delta Kappan,* vol. 76, no. 2, pp. 105–113, October 1994. Copyright © 1994 by Phi Delta Kappa. Reprinted with permission. All rights reserved.

Index

SkyLight
Training and Publishing Inc.

We Prepare Your Teachers Today for the Classrooms of Tomorrow

Learn from Our Books and from Our Authors!

Ignite Learning in Your School or District.

SkyLight's team of classroom-experienced consultants can help you foster systemic change for increased student achievement.

Professional development is a process, not an event. SkyLight's seasoned practitioners drive the creation of our on-site professional development programs, graduate courses, research-based publications, interactive video courses, teacher-friendly training materials, and online resources—call SkyLight Training and Publishing, Inc. today.

SkyLight specializes in three professional development areas.

Specialty #

Best Practices

We **model** the best practices that result in improved student performance and guided applications.

Specialty #

Making the Innovations Last

We help set up **support** systems that make innovations part of everyday practice in the long-term systemic improvement of your school or district.

Specialty #

How to Assess the Results

We prepare your school leaders to encourage and **assess** teacher growth, **measure** student achievement, and **evaluate** program success.

Contact the SkyLight team and begin a process toward long-term results.

SkyLight
Training and Publishing Inc.

2626 S. Clearbrook Dr., Arlington Heights, IL 60005
800-348-4474 • 847-290-6600 • FAX 847-290-6609

There are

one-story intellects,

two-story intellects, and three-story

intellects with skylights. All fact collectors, who

have no aim beyond their facts, are one-story men. Two-story men

compare, reason, generalize, using the labors of the fact collectors as

well as their own. Three-story men idealize, imagine,

predict—their best illumination comes from

above, through the skylight.

—*Oliver Wendell*

Holmes

SkyLight

Training and Publishing Inc.